T0288779

A

MARK TWAIN

CHRISTMAS

A JOURNEY ACROSS THREE CHRISTMAS SEASONS

BY CARLO DEVITO

CIDER MILL
PRESS

BOOK
PUBLISHERS

This book may be ordered by mail from the publisher. Please include $5.99 for postage and handling. Please support your local bookseller first!

Books published by Cider Mill Press Book Publishers are available at special discounts for bulk purchases in the United States by corporations, institutions, and other organizations. For more information, please contact the publisher.

Cider Mill Press Book Publishers
"Where good books are ready for press"
501 Nelson Place
Nashville, Tennessee 37214

cidermillpress.com

Typography: Copperplate, Goudy Old Style, Old Claude

Image Credits: See page 143

Printed in the United States of America

24 25 26 27 28 VER 6 5 4 3 2

This book is dedicated to my sons,
my family, friends, our dogs and
our cats, past and present.
Merry Christmas!

Contents

"It is my heart-warming and world-embracing
Christmas hope and aspiration that all of
us, the high, the low, the rich, the poor, the
admired, the despised, the loved, the hated, the
civilized, the savage (every man and brother
of us all throughout the whole earth), may
eventually be gathered together in a heaven of
everlasting rest and peace and bliss, except the
inventor of the telephone."

—*Mark Twain*, Boston Daily Globe

Introduction

How appropriate is it that as I sit here in rural New York during the winter holidays (a white Christmas this year, I might add) attempting to write this introduction, one of our many cats (Calli) insists on helping me by laying across my lap and then across my laptop? Twain loved cats. Luxurious as my lap is, I know she will desert me as soon as my wife enters the doorway, returning from her errands. The Christmas tree is decorated and lit. My children, now teenagers, are busying themselves with their presents and video games.

Several years ago, I visited the Mark Twain House during the Christmas season with my wife and our two young twin sons. The house on Farmington Avenue in Hartford, Connecticut, is beautiful throughout the year, but it was especially done up for the holidays when we were visiting. The boys attended under protest, and with our passing from one room to the next during the tour, they writhed in pain as if they were being stuck in their backs with forks that were being turned once plunged in. With every second that passed like Chinese water torture, their patience grew immeasurably thinner. I laughed, thinking Tom Sawyer or Huck Finn might have had the same reaction being taken through an old historical home. It's not an unlikely response for boys that age.

Somewhere, Mark Twain must have been laughing.

I first toured the house back in 1980 or 1981 with my parents. They loved visiting old historical houses, their favorites being in Newport, RI. But with my parents, any old house would do. I remember going through with the same horrible feeling my sons now had, asking repeatedly when we could leave. But still, the Twain House made an impression on me. I was a high school student at the time, and later an English major in college (a detail that obviously made no impression on me, as I commit murder of the language every day) where I read *Adventures of Huckleberry Finn* in one of my classes. I remember thinking that I could not help but be impressed. Of course, Twain had written *The Adventures of Tom Sawyer*, which was nice when I was a grammar school student. But as a college student I was stunned by his sense of irony, his facility with language, his ear for pronunciation, and the seriousness of the content. It suddenly dawned on me: Twain was a great writer! I carried this discovery around like I was the first one to find the New World. I had discovered Mark Twain! My professors were horrified and amused by my sincere proclamations marked by a sheer lack of worldliness.

Again, I think Twain himself would have been amused.

I remember thinking how wonderful the house looked. The tour made a huge impression on me.

One could not help but imagine Twain's chattering three daughters, Susy, Clara, and Jean, squealing about the house amidst the festive decorations in anticipation of the holiday season. One can practically see Twain himself walking about the house amid the holiday madness he accused his wife Livy of fomenting. But, of course, Twain was a classic enabler when it came to the season.

Samuel Clemens, the man behind the pen name Mark Twain, loved his family. He loved his large home in Hartford. And for all his humorous protestations and posing, he loved Christmas. His wife Livy, whom he adored, loved Christmas even more. And Christmas remained with him, like a haunting ghost, long after the golden days had passed and the children had grown up, when the family no longer lived at the Farmington Avenue residence. Even in later years, when old age had sapped his strength, he held on tightly to those memories, as did his daughters. Christmas in the Clemens home was in fact a magical time.

That is part of the magic of Twain's story and the magic of Christmas. It's hectic and messy and expensive, and there's worry and joy and argument. And we do it all over again every twelve months! But it is a shared madness. It is something we all have in common—the joyful experiences and the lifelong memories.

Family is the connective tissue that makes Christmas such an important season for each and every one of us. Twain had many festive Christmases with his family, most of them in the Farmington Avenue home where they lived from 1874 to 1891. In discovering more about Twain and Christmas, he, like everyone, also had his share of sorrow. I found great humor and pathos in three of Twain's Christmas seasons. The first, Twain's penultimate holiday in 1908, is a snapshot that perfectly captures his famous wit and wisdom. The 1875 season paints a perfect picture of Christmas cheer. And Twain's last Christmas in 1909 reveals the humanity in America's greatest writer.

In preparation for this book, I asked my sons to accompany me back to the Twain House this past Christmas, 2012. Of course I had to bribe them. Two-foot-long hot dogs at Doogie's restaurant in

Newington, right down the road, was the agreed upon price for their acquiescence.

As we toured the home again, there was less writhing. My sons, now teenagers, instead pointed out things with a sense of fascination. Little things. Children's ABC blocks in the nursery. Details in Susy's room. They laughed at several stories told by the college-aged young man who was our tour guide. They envied Twain's huge office complete with desk and pool table. As the guide told stories of Twain and his friends smoking cigars, drinking, and playing pool, my sons chided me that they would be more interested in books if my office more resembled Twain's. Suddenly, Twain, this irascible, cigar-chomping comedian, was interesting to them. And to my surprise, there was no rush to leave. We even spent some time in the gift shop buying books, without complaint. Afterwards we went to Doogie's, as promised, and scarfed down hot dogs and fries and washed them down with sodas.

On the car ride home, I remember looking into the rearview mirror of our minivan expecting to find my sons asleep. Instead, I noticed one of them reading a Mark Twain quote book, and laughing. And I thought to myself, "Now there's a Christmas present."

And then I thought, well, somewhere Twain must be laughing once again.

Carlo DeVito
December 25, 2012

1908

The Elephant in the Room

In December of 1908, Robert J. Collier had sent a letter to Twain at Stormfield informing him that a large Christmas present—a baby elephant!—was on its way.

Robert Joseph Collier was the son of Peter Fenelon Collier, and a principal in the publishing company P. F. Collier & Son. His father, the founder, was originally born in Ireland and had immigrated to Ohio in 1866. Peter Collier first published a series of books aimed at Roman Catholics, but soon expanded his empire. He founded *Collier's Once a Week* in April 1888. It was advertised as a magazine of "fiction, fact, sensation, wit, humor, news". By 1892, *Collier's Once a Week* had a circulation of over 250,000 and was one of the largest-selling magazines in the United States. In 1895, the name was changed to *Collier's Weekly: An Illustrated Journal*.

Robert J. Collier, a graduate of Georgetown, took over as publisher of *Collier's Weekly* after his father's death in 1909, and became the magazine's editor after Norman Hapgood left for *Harper's Weekly* in 1912. Circulation continued to grow, and by 1917 it had reached one million. As president of the Aero Club of America, he was as keen about publishing as he was about flying. Collier, a friend of Orville Wright and a director of the Wright Company, purchased a Wright Model B aircraft in 1911 and loaned it to the United States Army. The Army used this aircraft to fly along the Rio Grande border of Mexico and the United States in one of the first scouting duties by the U.S. Army using an airplane.

Collier added in his letter that the baby elephant, Twain's Christmas present, would be sent as soon as he could reserve a rail car for it. The Barnum & Bailey Circus headquarters in Bridgeport, Connecticut, was loaning Collier a keeper to oversee the transport and delivery of the animal to his friend.

Mark Twain at Stormfield.

"The news created a disturbance in Stormfield," wrote Twain biographer Albert Bigelow Paine. "One could not refuse, discourteously and abruptly, a costly present like that; but it seemed a disaster to accept it. An elephant would require a roomy and warm place, also a variety of attention which Stormfield was not prepared to supply. . . . There was no good place to put an elephant in Stormfield."

At the ripe old age of seventy-three years, Mark Twain had quit New York City in October of 1908, satisfied to spend his last days at his Italianate villa, Stormfield. The piece of property Twain had settled on in Redding, Connecticut, was isolated and suffered extreme weather at times. "Twain bought the expansive property sight unseen and asked not to be saddled with the construction plans. All he wanted was space for an orchestrelle and a red billiard room, and the rest he left up to his daughter, Clara, and his secretary, Isabel Lyon," journalist Alyssa Karas wrote.

"On the 18th of June, 1908, at about four in the afternoon we left New York City by an express train that was to make its first stop in Redding that day," recorded a young Louise Paine, daughter of Albert Bigelow Paine. "With Mr. Clemens were my father, a reporter or two, a photographer and that most fortunate little girl, myself, whose boarding school closed that day so that I, too, was homeward bound to Redding."

Any time Twain moved, it was noteworthy in the media, and this was no exception. However, this was as much fanfare as the small little wayward town saw on any Fourth of July. "Waiting for us at the Redding station was a proud array of carriages, flower trimmed, and filled with smiling people who waved warmly. I knew I would never forget it. Mr. Clemens waved in return, then stepped into his own carriage and drove toward the beautiful house that was to be his last home," remembered Louise.

"Do you like it here at Stormfield?" asked a correspondent from the *New York Times* of his new home that same month.

"Yes, it is the most out of the world and peaceful and tranquil and in every way satisfactory home I have had experience of in my life," answered Twain without sarcasm.

Twain liked his house and it filled his correspondence. He wrote to Dorothy Quick, a friend, just a day after his arrival, "I was never in this beautiful region until yesterday evening. Miss Lyon and the architect built and furnished the house without any help or advice from me, and the result is entirely to my satisfaction. It is charmingly quiet here. The house stands alone, with nothing in sight but woodsy hills and rolling country."

Stormfield, in Redding, Connecticut.

Twain wrote to William Dean Howells on August 12, 1908, "Won't you and Mrs. Howells and Mildred come and give us as many days as you can spare, and examine John's triumph? It is the most satisfactory house I am acquainted with, and the most satisfactorily situated. But it is no place to work in, because one is outside of it all the time, while the sun and the moon are on duty. Outside of it in the loggia, where the breezes blow and the tall arches divide up the scenery and frame it.

"It's a ghastly long distance to come, and I wouldn't travel such a distance to see anything short of a memorial museum, but if you can't come now you can at least come later when you return to New York, for the journey will be only an hour and a half per express-train. Things are gradually and steadily taking shape inside the house, and nature is taking care of the outside in her ingenious and wonderful fashion—and she is competent and asks no help and gets none. I have retired from New York for good, I have retired from labor for good, I have dismissed my stenographer and have entered upon a holiday whose other end is in the cemetery."

"Not that he was really old; he never was that. His step, his manner, his point of view, were all and always young," Paine wrote. "He was fond of children and frequently had them about him. He delighted in games—especially in billiards—and in building the house at Stormfield the billiard-room was first considered. He had a genuine passion for the sport; without it his afternoon was not complete. His mornings he was likely to pass in bed, smoking—he was always smoking—and attending to his correspondence and reading. History and the sciences interested him, and his bed was strewn with biographies and stories of astronomical and geological research. The vastness of distances and periods always impressed him. He had no head for figures, but he would labor for hours over scientific calculations, trying to compass them and to grasp their gigantic import."

Paine remembered having found Twain quite delighted with himself for having "figured out for himself the length in hours and minutes of a 'light year.' He showed me the pages covered with figures, and was more proud of them than if they had been the pages of an immortal story. Then we played billiards, but even his favorite game could not make him altogether forget his splendid achievement."

"While living at Stormfield, Twain decided the town needed a library," Karas wrote. "He placed a collection sign on his mantel and pressed Stormfield male visitors to donate a dollar to his cause. The library opened in late 1910, after Twain's death, and still operates today. Before his death, Twain donated a collection of about 1,000 books as a core collection to a temporary library." To this day some volumes remain at the present library. There is also a fun collection of bric-a-brac, such as his old and much-loved billiard balls, a traveling cigar case, and a homemade writing table.

In September of 1909, two professional burglars broke into Twain's house. Miss Lyons was the first to hear the commotion, but the two escaped the estate with their booty. Lyons called the Sherriff and Harry A. Lounsbury, who was a neighbor and a close friend in Twain's last days.

The burglary made national news. The *New York Times* reported, "Mr. Lounsbury and Deputy Sheriff Banks found peculiar footprints, which they followed to Bethel. Mr. Lounsbury discovered the men on the train in the smoking car. He attempted to engage them in conversation and asked them if they lived in Danbury. The men replied vaguely. Mr. Lounsbury said he noticed that both men's shoes had rubber heels, which it was said would correspond with the tracks in the roadway. When the train arrived at Redding Mr. Lounsbury got off and notified Banks that he believed the men they were after were the two to whom he had been talking. Banks boarded the train, and when an attempt was made to arrest the burglars one ran out of the car door and jumped off and the other showed fight and drew a revolver. He fired four shots, one of which struck the Sheriff in the leg, and one, the last in the struggle, hit the burglar himself in the head. A passenger jumped into the fight and subdued the burglar with a club, cutting his head open. The burglar who jumped was found under a bridge in Brookside Park. A physician was called and the wounds of the Sheriff and of the injured robber were attended to."

The incident drew quite a stir, and Lounsbury, Twain, Clara, and Miss Lyons all had to attend the sentencing. Twain posted this note on the front door of the house:

Notice. To the next Burglar.

There is nothing but plated ware in this house, now and henceforth. You will find it in that brass thing in the dining-room over in the corner by the basket of kittens. If you want the basket, put the kittens in the brass thing. Do not make a noise—it disturbs the family. You will find rubbers in the front hall, by that thing which has the umbrellas in it, chiffonier, I think they call it, or pergola, or something like that. Please close the door when you go away!

Very Truly Yours,
S. L. CLEMENS.

Thus, after the burglary, the elephant's arrival would be yet another strange incident to occur in Twain's new house less than a few months of his taking residence there. Twain hated telephones, so his secretary was dispatched to intercede.

"Oh, put him in the garage," Collier told Twain's secretary, Isabelle Lyon.

"But there's no heat in the garage," responded the flustered and nervous Ms. Lyon.

"Well, put him in the loggia, then. That's closed in, isn't it, for the winter? Plenty of sunlight—just the place for a young elephant," said Collier.

"But we play cards in the loggia," said the flustered secretary. "We use it for a sort of sun-parlor."

"But that wouldn't matter. He's a kindly, playful little thing. He'll be just like a kitten. I'll send the man up to look over the place and tell you just how to take care of him, and I'll send up several bales of hay in advance. It isn't a large elephant, you know: just a little one—a regular plaything," concluded the publisher of one of America's bestselling magazines. Ms. Lyon was at her wit's end.

"There was nothing further to be done; only to wait and dread until the Christmas present's arrival," Paine recalled. "A few days before Christmas ten bales of hay arrived and several bushels of carrots. This store of provender aroused no enthusiasm at Stormfield. It would seem there was no escape now."

Paine wrote, "On Christmas morning Mr. Lounsbury telephoned up that there was a man at the station who said he was an elephant-trainer from Barnum & Bailey's, sent by Mr. Collier to look at the elephant's quarters and get him settled when he should arrive. Orders were given to bring the man over. The day of doom was at hand.

"It isn't a large elephant, you know: just a little one—a regular plaything."

"But Lounsbury's detective instinct came once more into play. He had seen a good many elephant-trainers at Bridgeport, and he thought this one had a doubtful look.

" 'Where is the elephant?' Harry Lounsbury asked, as they drove along.

" 'He will arrive at noon.'

" 'Where are you going to put him?'

" 'In the loggia,' said the trainer.

" 'How big is he?'

" 'About the size of a cow.'

" 'How long have you been with Barnum and Bailey?'

" 'Six years.'

" 'Then you must know some friends of mine' (naming two that had no existence until that moment).

" 'Oh yes, indeed. I know them well.'

"Lounsbury didn't say any more just then, but he had a feeling that perhaps the dread at Stormfield had grown unnecessarily large. Something told him that this man seemed rather more like a butler, or a valet, than an elephant-trainer. They drove to Stormfield, and the trainer looked over the place. It would do perfectly, he said. He gave a few instructions as to the care of this new household feature, and was driven back to the station to bring it," recorded Paine.

"Lounsbury came back by and by, bringing the elephant but not the trainer," Paine wrote. "It didn't need a trainer. It was a beautiful specimen, with soft, smooth coat and handsome trappings, perfectly quiet, well-behaved and small—suited to the loggia, as Collier had said—for it was only two feet long and beautifully made of cloth and cotton—one of the fairest toy elephants ever seen anywhere."

Twain loved the deception, and marveled at his friend's gag.

Twain wrote Robert Collier, threatening revenge for letting the beast loose on his estate, declaring that the elephant was devastating Stormfield.

"To send an elephant in a trance, under pretense that it was dead or stuffed!" Twain wrote. "The animal came to life, as you knew it would, and began to observe Christmas, and we now have no furniture left and no servants and no visitors, no friends, no photographs, no burglars—nothing but the elephant. Be kind, be merciful, be generous; take him away and send us what is left of the earthquake."

Not to be outdone, Collier retorted to Twain that he thought it unkind of him to look a gift-elephant in the trunk!

1875

Santa's Footprint

On a cold, crisp December day in 1875—Christmas Day, in fact—Sam Clemens walked down Farmington Avenue in Hartford, Connecticut, savoring his cigar. He was lean, with a bushy head of black hair and a bushy mustache to match. He chewed on his cigar, moved it from one side of his mouth to the other, and looked proudly at the home he and his wife Livy had built. The home was adorned with large green wreaths in all the downstairs windows, and a giant green wreath placed proudly on the upper pane of the prominent wooden front door welcomed visitors through the threshold and into the inner sanctum of their warm, inviting large home.

Twain loved the Christmas season, and reveled in its luxuries as much as its obvious foibles. Outwardly, he presented his usual sarcastic, corkscrew insights about the holiday, lampooning its failures at any chance.

Twain in the 1870s.

"The approach of Christmas brings harassment and dread to many excellent people. They have to buy a cart-load of presents, and they never know what to buy to hit the various tastes; they put in three weeks of hard and anxious work, and when Christmas morning comes they are so dissatisfied with the result, and so disappointed that they want to sit down and cry. Then they give thanks that Christmas comes but once a year," Clemens would later write in *Following the Equator*. He also poked fun at the New Year's celebration as "a harmless annual institution, of no particular use to anybody save as a scapegoat for promiscuous drunks, and friendly calls and humbug resolutions."

But in reality, Clemens was as susceptible to the season's charms as anyone. He and Livy were generous to a fault, especially around the holidays, and took great pains and experienced great joy indulging each other and their children in all the thrills of the season. Sam had worked hard this year, and he was determined that his young family would have an exceptional Christmas. As usual, his beautiful wife Livy had spent herself buying and wrapping presents for many weeks, and he had his own little surprise planned for his family. It was something that would leave an indelible mark not only for his children, but for generations to come.

Clara, Jean, Livy, and Susy.

"Samuel Clemens had spent much of 1875, his fortieth year, absorbed in adult concerns. Yet in certain ways, this year had also restored him powerfully to his youthful past," wrote Twain biographer Ron Powers. "And then on Christmas morning, he out did himself. . . ."

As Sam walked alone on Christmas morning, he ruminated on recent events he had read about in the newspapers. He scanned follow-up stories about the November 4th collision between the naval vessels *Pacific* and *Orpheus* off Cape Flattery, Washington, in which 236 people had perished. And he was fully up to date on the return to prison of William Marcy "Boss" Tweed, of the Tammany Hall political machine, in the beginning of December. Tweed had dramatically escaped from jail and fled the country. It turned out that Tweed had fled to Cuba and then Spain where he was identified from cartoons by Clemens' good friend, Thomas Nast, and eventually returned home via armed guard. And of course, Clemens had read about the violent bread riots in Montreal on December 17.

He was relieved to be up and about, since he had been fighting a bout of dysentery during the last weeks of the year. It had so plagued him, that his discomforts had found voice in his letters, though his sense of humor had not deserted him. In one missive to Reverend Joseph Twichell, whom Clemens regarded as a close friend, he scribbled, "Question: If a Congress of Presbyterians is a PRESBYtery, what is a Congress of dysenters?"

Despite the physical setback, as he approached the house with his usual gait, Clemens could not have helped but wonder how had he made it this far—from loitering around the slave quarters on his uncle's farm in Missouri before the Civil War, to this place of wealth and success now. How had it all come so fast? How had it all fallen together so quickly?

Just less than a decade earlier, in 1865, Sam experienced his first "big break," which came on the heels of the publication of his short story, "Jim Smiley and His Jumping Frog," which had appeared in newspapers all across the country. Within a year of its publication, the *Sacramento Union* newspaper in California hired Sam to visit and report on the Sandwich Islands (now known as Hawaii). The articles earned a loyal following, which Twain discovered upon his return. From there his fame skyrocketed as he trod the boards as a lecture-tour celebrity.

The still single Sam had arrived in New York City in 1867, on assignment for the newspaper *Alta California* to write travel essays from the East Coast for readers back on the West Coast who looked to the San Francisco paper for news and entertainment. From that port city, he steamed to Europe and then the Holy Land. His vivid descriptions and candid, if not downright hilarious, observations of life in faraway lands confirmed him as a writer of the first rank, and as a great humorist. He quickly became a national celebrity. His new position in the American literary firmament was confirmed with the publication of his first book, *Innocents Abroad*, in 1869.

While traveling, Clemens met his future brother-in-law, Charles Langdon, who reportedly showed Sam a picture of his sister, Olivia, and Sam fell in love at first sight. Sam met and courted Olivia Langdon (her friends, family, and Clemens called her "Livy") for two years. Clemens adored Livy. In 1870, they married and moved to the town of Buffalo, New York, where Sam had become a partner, editor, and writer for the daily newspaper the *Buffalo Express*. As a wedding present, Livy's father gave them a large, well-to-do house. While living in Buffalo, their first child, Langdon Clemens, was born.

"In 1871, Sam moved his family to Hartford, Connecticut, a city he had come to love while visiting his publisher there, and where he had made friends. Livy also had family connections to the city. For the first few years the Clemenses rented a house in the heart of Nook Farm, a residential area that was home to numerous writers, publishers and other prominent figures. In 1872, Sam's recollections and tall tales from his frontier adventures were published in his book, *Roughing It*. That same year the Clemenses' first daughter Susy was born, but their son, Langdon, died at the age of [nineteen months] from diphtheria," wrote Mark Twain House historians Patti Philippon and Beatrice Fox Auerbach.

Sam and Livy soon bought land on Farmington Avenue, and in 1873 they hired New York architect Edward Tuckerman Potter to design their house.

"Livy had strong opinions about the design of her home; she drew sketches and sought the counsel of trusted friends on her ideas," Philippon and Auerbach wrote. "Construction began in August 1873, while Sam and Livy were abroad. Although there was still much finish work to be completed, the family moved into their house on September 19, 1874."

The Clemens home on Farmington Avenue in Hartford, Connecticut.

The sprawling, multi-gabled twenty-five-room house was designed in the High Victorian Gothic style by Edward Tuckerman Potter (who was known for his churches, including the Church of the Good Shepherd). Livy was the one primarily involved in planning with the architect—apparently all Sam Clemens asked for was a red brick house!

There was also a servant's wing and a carriage house. Sam and Livy employed about seven or so servants, including his butler, George Griffin (of whom Sam was personally fond), maid Katy Leary and coachman Patrick McAleer. Construction delays and the ever-increasing costs of building their dream home frustrated Sam. In spite of this, Sam was enamored with the finished product, saying, "It is a home—& the word never had so much meaning before."

Sam Clemens and his family enjoyed what the author would later call the happiest and most productive years of his life in their Hartford home. He wrote, "To us, our house . . . had a heart, and a soul, and eyes to see us with, and approvals and solicitudes and deep sympathies; it was of us, and we were in its confidence and lived in its grace and in the peace of its benediction."

This would be, without question, the high point of Clemens' personal and family life. Clemens lived in this house from 1874-1891 with his wife and their three daughters, Suzy, Clara, and Jean. It was while living here that Clemens wrote many of his great classic works such as *The Adventures of Tom Sawyer*, *Adventures of Huckleberry Finn*, and *A Connecticut Yankee in King Arthur's Court*.

As Clemens approached his house on Christmas morning, 1875, he thought on his wife's recent birthday, that late November, and how much he cherished her presence in his life. Sam's letters to his wife were filled with adoration. He thought her exceptionally pretty and smart.

Olivia Louise Langdon was born on November 27, 1845, in Elmira, New York. She was the daughter of Jervis and Olivia Langdon. She had a younger brother, Charles, and an adopted older sister, Susan. She married Samuel Clemens on February 2, 1870.

Livy's family was well-to-do, and she had been well educated. She had studied Latin, arithmetic, English, grammar, American history, music, and philosophy at the Elmira Female College where she began her studies at the age of twelve. "She was 14 when her health became so fragile that she had to stop attending school. Even during the ensuing years of treatment, Olivia sought to educate herself with determination. She had tutors; she put together study groups and for a time a professor from the college came to the Langdon home for her lessons," wrote Rebecca Floyd of the Mark Twain House.

One of Olivia's close friends, Alice Hooker of Hartford, wrote: "[Livy] is so much more thoughtful, original, deep, than most girls and so is constantly making me go to the foundations of things."

Sam Clemens wrote about his future wife to his sister in 1869: "I take as much pride in her brains as I do in her beauty, & as much pride in her happy & equable disposition as I do in her brains."

Before Sam met Livy, she spent time in multiple health treatment centers in Elmira, Washington D.C., and New York City. In retrospect we know today that Olivia was suffering from Pott's disease, or tuberculosis of the spine. She was fortunate enough to receive treatment from the country's leading physicians on diseases of the spine in New York City.

"Sam Clemens entered Olivia's life in the time not long after her health began to improve. . . ." Floyd wrote. "After they returned from the tour, Charles invited Clemens to dine with the Langdon family in New York City. Little is known of that first meeting. A few days later, New Year's Day, Clemens called on Livy at the house where she was staying. Rather than stay the socially acceptable 15 minutes, he stayed for 12 hours. During the summer of 1868 the Langdons invited Clemens to visit their home in Elmira, during which time Clemens' feelings for Olivia deepened. Although it took some time, eventually Olivia reciprocated Sam's devotions. Their courtship, marriage and love for one another are much documented in the correspondence they exchanged throughout their marriage.

"Like the relationship between her own parents, Livy's and Sam's marriage was very much one of equals. Deeds to their house and land in Hartford were in Olivia's name. For a time Mark Twain's copyrights were transferred to her to preserve the family income from creditors. Olivia was also an active participant in her husband's writing. He left pages of manuscript by her bedside for her to read and review. He often, though not always, accepted her suggestions. Visitors in the Mark Twain House today hear the story of how the children would sit by Mama as she read Papa's writing, and how she would turn down the pages when she saw something that needed more work. Susy and Clara would cry out because Mama wanted to cut out some of the parts the girls thought were most 'delectable.' Clemens remembered in his autobiography how he liked to insert phrases and incidents which he knew Olivia would not approve—just to see her reaction."

And Clemens was devoted to her. "I feel ashamed of my idleness, and yet I have had really no inclination to do anything but court Livy. . . . She is only a little body, but she hasn't her peer in Christendom," gushed Twain in letters to his sister Jane Clemens and family in 1868. "She is a splendid girl. She spends no money but her usual year's allowance, and she spends nearly every cent of that on other people. She will be a good sensible little wife, without any airs about her. I don't make intercession for her beforehand and ask you to love her, for there isn't any use in that—you couldn't help it if you were to try. I warn you that whoever comes within the fatal influence of her beautiful nature is her willing slave for evermore."

Olivia Langdon Clemens.

In November of 1875, Livy had turned thirty years old. Twain wrote to Livy on her birthday:

To Mrs. Clemens on her Thirtieth Birthday:

HARTFORD, November 27, 1875.

Livy darling, six years have gone by since I made my first great success in life and won you, and thirty years have passed since Providence made preparation for that happy success by sending you into the world. Every day we live together adds to the security of my confidence, that we can never any more wish to be separated than that we can ever imagine a regret that we were ever joined. You are dearer to me to-day, my child, than you were upon the last anniversary of this birth-day; you were dearer then than you were a year before—you have grown more and more dear from the first of those anniversaries, and I do not doubt that this precious progression will continue on to the end.

Let us look forward to the coming anniversaries, with their age and their gray hairs without fear and without depression, trusting and believing that the love we bear each other will be sufficient to make them blessed.

So, with abounding affection for you and our babies, I hail this day that brings you the matronly grace and dignity of three decades!

Always Yours
S. L. C.

"Mother wore very beautiful dresses that I remember as distinctly now as if they had been lovely pictures in a gallery," Clara Clemens remembered many years later. "Father noticed and enjoyed Mother's clothes, but rarely when they were new."

"Livy, what a beautiful dress that is," Sam would say.

"Mother had been wearing the same gown for six months at least. It always amused her," scribbled Clara.

For her part, Livy was enamored of Sam, and often bade him home when he was off traveling. Her pet name for Sam was "Youth."

"When my thoughts return to childhood, I see figures of romance moving in the atmosphere of fairyland," remembered Clara many years later. "There was something romantic, even dramatic, about the atmosphere of this home of ours in Hartford, Connecticut. It was a brick building with many little turrets, porches, and towers."

"Father never showed the least sign of being bored when my sister Suzy and I clambered upon his knee, begging for a 'long' story," Clara wrote, describing life with her father. "Father was always ready to make jokes at the breakfast table, and my impression is that his wit was not half appreciated at that hour of the morning. . . . I would say that my father was the only one at the table who found any real joy in life so early in the morning. . . .

"In spite of a very full life, my father found time for his three little girls, and thought of many ways to amuse them. After a visit to Montreal, where he and my mother were entertained by the Viceroy, he returned with not only the gayest-colored toboggan costumes from my sisters and me, but a full-sized toboggan. At the same time he supplied us with three collies that we christened, 'I know,' 'You know,' and 'Don't know.'

"A toboggan slide had to be arranged behind the house, but this was not difficult, as our home stood on the top of a small hill that sloped gradually to a rather broad meadow bounded on the far side by a river. Father was as jubilant as any of us the first day we gathered on the crest of the hill to try the new toboggan. Viewed from the street at a distance of forty yards, we must have formed a bright picture on that sparkling winter's day—three small girls in their blue, yellow, and red costumes surrounded by three gamboling dogs, directed by a picturesque man dressed in a sealskin coat with a cap drawn down over his curly gray hair. The dogs barked so loudly, and the children laughed so much, that I doubt Father's explanations of the art of tobogganing were much appreciated."

There was a ravine down below and behind the large house. "Father also taught us to skate on the little river that flowed through the meadow behind the house, and often we glided back and forth on the white ice until the sun had set and the trees looked like giant specters. Then the stars came out and the lights of our 'castle' beckoned us home, a home that was filled with cheer," remembered daughter Clara. "Not infrequently we awoke to find the many trees behind our house one mass of dazzling ice. Each branch and twig glistened with beauty and absorbed the attention of the entire family."

But if anything, Twain was in love with his daughters, writing proudly, "They say God made man in his own effigy. I don't know about that, but I am quite sure he put a lot of divinity into the American girl."

Clara, Jean, and Susy Clemens with their dog, Hash.

All three girls were very pretty. Susy, the oldest, was bright, forthright, outspoken, and outgoing. Twain fell in love with her and remained enamored of her his whole life. There was a lot of Sam in Susy. He called her "Wee wifie" and "Megalopis" (suggested by her great, dark eyes). Clara was more even-tempered, and in later years was his literary protector. Jean, the baby of the family, was frail and gentle. She battled epilepsy her entire life, with bouts of severe illness and small runs of seemingly good health. Nonetheless, she was adored.

Twain had two habits: cigars and billiards.

"Smoke? I always smoke from 3 till 5 on Sunday afternoons—and in New York the other day I smoked a week, day & night. But when Livy is well I smoke only those two hours on Sunday. I'm 'boss' of the habit, now, & shall never let it boss me any-more. Originally, I quit solely on Livy's account, (not that I believed there was the faintest reason in the matter, but just as I would deprive myself of sugar in my coffee if she wished it, or quit wearing socks if she thought them immoral), & I stick to it yet on Livy's account, and shall always continue to do so, without a pang," Clemens wrote to close friend Reverend Twichell on December 19, 1870. ". . . Ah, it is turning one's back upon a kindly Providence to spurn away from us the good crea-ture he sent to make the breath of life a luxury as well as a necessity, enjoyable as well as useful, to go and quit smoking when there ain't any sufficient excuse for it! Why, my old boy, when they use to tell me I would shorten my life ten years by smoking, they little knew the devotee they were wasting their puerile word upon—they little knew how trivial and valueless I would regard a decade that had no smoking in it! But I won't persuade you, Twichell—I won't until I see you again—but then we'll smoke for a week together, and then shut off again."

"He smokes a great deal almost incessantly," Susy Clemens wrote while in her teens. "His favorite game is billiards and when he is tired, and wishes to rest himself he stays up all night and plays billiards, it seems to rest his head."

The billiard room served as Mark Twain's office, study, and private domain. Located on the third floor, away from the bustle of a busy household, it was the place where the author would write many of his great works, fanning the manuscripts on the billiard table to be edited. Twain could relax and informally entertain friends, sometimes into the early morning hours. The billiard table now in the house was given to Sam by a friend in 1904.

"Every Friday evening, or oftener, a small party of billiard-lovers gathered, and played until a late hour, told stories, and smoked until the room was blue, comforting themselves with Scotch and general good fellowship.," remembered Paine. "He

never tired of the game. He could play all night. He could stay until the last man gave out from sheer weariness; then he would go on knocking the balls about alone. He liked to invent new games and new rules for old games, often inventing rules on the spur of the moment to fit some particular shot or position on the table. It amused him highly to do this, to make the rule advantage his own play, and to pretend a deep indignation when his opponents disqualified his rulings and rode him down."

"I wonder why a man should prefer a good billiard-table to a poor one; and why he should prefer straight cues to crooked ones; and why he should prefer round balls to chipped ones; and why he should prefer a level table to one that slants; and why he should prefer responsive cushions to the dull and unresponsive kind. I wonder at these things, because when we examine the matter we find that the essentials involved in billiards are as competently and exhaustively furnished by a bad billiard outfit as they are by the best one. One of the essentials is amusement. Very well, if there is any more amusement to be gotten out of the one outfit than out of the other, the facts are in favor of the bad outfit," Twain wrote a friend later in life.

Twain had recently seen a tournament of "billiard champions of world-wide fame contend against each other, and certainly the art and science displayed were a wonder to see; yet I saw nothing there in the way of science and art that was more wonderful than shots which I had seen Texas Tom make on the wavy surface of that poor old wreck in the perishing saloon at Jackass Gulch forty years before," Paine wrote.

Katy Leary, the Clemenses' loyal housekeeper, described one such incident in this fashion: "Mr. Clemens spent most of his time up in the billiard room, writing or playing billiards. One day when I went in, and he was shooting the balls around the table, I noticed smoke coming up from the hearth. I called Patrick, and John O'Neill, the gardener, and we began taking up the hearth to see what was the matter. Mr. Clemens kept on playing billiards right along and paid no attention to what we were doing. Finally, when we got the hearth up, flame and smoke came out into the room. The house was on fire. Mr. Clemens noticed then what we were about, and went over to the corner where there were some bottle fire extinguishers. He took one down and threw it into the flames. This put them out a good deal, and he took up his cue, went back to the table and began to shoot the balls around again as if nothing had happened. Mrs. Clemens came in just then and said, 'Why the house is afire!' "

" 'Yes, I know it,' he replied, but went on playing."

After one outburst of temper while playing pool, Twain turned to his biographer, Albert Bigelow Paine, and said apologetically, "This is a most amusing game. When you play badly it amuses me, and when I play badly and lose my temper, it certainly must amuse you."

Playing billiards and hiding in his office as he might try, for Twain there was no escaping the Christmas holidays and his own generous nature.

"Both father and mother had the right feeling about bestowing financial help. They well realized that pleasure in giving was only possible if one's gift was unaccompanied by the least desire for gratitude or even recognition in return," recalled Clara. "They gave because they enjoyed helping an unfortunate man or woman, and for no other reason.

"I shall never forget the royal preparations for Christmas tide in our home. At that time I appreciated everything, chiefly as a thrilling experience that made up for the trials endured during school hours. But how could any one individual buy, wrap up, and expedite so many presents for one single day in the year as my mother did? Presents for the family, for the servants, for poor children and their parents, for friends abroad, for the sick and insane."

By contrast, Clemens' boyhood Christmases were somewhat less opulent and more reminiscent of scenes from *The Adventures of Tom Sawyer*. "In June, 1835, John M. Clemens arrived with his family and Jennie, the housemaid, in the little frontier village of Florida, Missouri, where they were met and greeted by their kinspeople. Here only a few months later, on November 30, 1835, Mrs. Clemens gave birth to the son, Samuel Langhorne [Clemens]," wrote historian Donald H. Welsh.

"The churches . . . assumed leadership in the observance of Christmas. At the Methodist Church the Sunday school met on Christmas Day at 9 a.m. for a hymn, a lecture by Thomas Sunderland, an address by the Reverend Mr. Marvin, distribution of refreshments, and a closing hymn. The *Gazette* reported that many were present, that it was a pleasure to look upon their 'smiling, happy faces, and witness their demonstrations of pleasure,' and that 'good order was preserved throughout,' " Welsh reported.

"The holiday season provided a period of special activity. Events scheduled for December, 1847, included the Christmas ball and supper, music lessons being given to a class in the City Hotel 'by Mr. Coinski, an accomplished musician,' Monday night meetings of the sewing society formed by the Methodist ladies for the purpose of purchasing chandeliers for the church, the singing class at the schoolhouse on Saturday evenings and the Sons of Temperance lectures on Saturday evenings," Welsh continued.

During the "season of fun and jollity, of hot punches and temperance processions, of sermons and balls, of praying and feasting, the mayor held open house on Christmas day for the reception of visitors and the extension of 'lots of good cheer,' the Palmyra and Hannibal Sons of Temperance joined to form a procession to the Baptist Church for a sermon and the ladies held open house on New Year's Day for the purpose of receiving calls: 'Hospitable and agreeable at all times, on that day they will be peculiarly so to all who will avail themselves of the opportunity afforded by this good old social custom, to renew or extend their acquaintance.'

"The wealthier citizens staged many social events in the name of charity. In November, 1846, the ladies held a dinner in Hawkins' Saloon, feeding over 100 at 50£ each, the receipts to go for the relief of destitute families," Welsh wrote.

"On Christmas night 150 enjoyed a ball held in Hawkins' Saloon for the benefit of widows and orphans, gentlemen's tickets selling at $2," Welsh continued. "Children were allowed at these affairs, as the editor noted that 'Among the dancers we observed two or three little sylphs, from seven to ten years of age, who moved with fairy lightness and grace, as if to dance was the only motion they knew.' "

However, in Hartford, the Twain entrance hall provided an appropriately impressive area for receiving visitors. Leon Marcotte of New York and Paris carved the entrance hall's ornamental detail when the house was built. In 1881, the interior design firm of Louis C. Tiffany & Co., Associated Artists, was hired to stencil the room's original wainscoting in silver, and paint the walls and ceiling red with patterns of black and silver. They drew inspiration from other cultures such as the Middle East and Asia to form a cohesive design scheme that flowed throughout the first floor and public spaces of the house.

In the years the Clemens lived in Hartford, the house was richly appointed during the holidays. In Clemens' day, the front hall would be highly decorated. Light would twinkle off the silver stenciling draped around the room. Fantastic greenery was meticulously placed on the mantle and above each doorway. The fresh scent of evergreen boughs was everywhere, filling the house with holiday spirit. Baskets for the poor were stored in the front hall and handed out on Christmas Eve day.

The Christmas tree in the main parlor was festooned with decorations made by the girls—Susy, Clara, and Jean. Paper ornaments, crochet snowflakes, popcorn and cranberry garlands, and tinsel adorned the tree. Sam, and later the girls, loved playing the piano and singing Christmas carols. Sing-alongs were part of the Clemens family Christmas rituals, with classic holiday songs and hymns part of the family repertoire.

Like other American families, the Clemenses took pride in their holiday table settings. Of course, theirs were more opulent than many. At the center of the table was an exquisite silver epergne centerpiece, a gift from their wedding.

Sam was as generous with Livy as he could possibly be, and showered her with loving letters. "Joy, and peace be with you and about you, and the benediction of God rest upon you this day! . . . There is something beautiful about all that old hollowed Christmas legend! It mellows a body—it warms the torpid kindnesses and charities into life. And so I hail my darling, with a great, big, whole-hearted Christmas blessing. God be and abide with her evermore."

In late 1875, Twain had purchased an ornate brass fender for the fireplace in the entryway of their house. A fender is a low metal wall placed on the hearthstone at the bottom of the fireplace, which stops any coals or firewood from falling out of the roaring fire and onto the carpet or wooden floor. Twain decided to make a surprise gift of it to Livy for Christmas.

"You can't imagine how brilliant and beautiful that new brass fender is, and how perfectly naturally it takes its place under the carved oak. How they did scour it up before they sent it! I lied a good deal about it when I came home—so for once I kept a secret and surprised Livy on a Christmas morning!," an excited Twain wrote to friend William Dean Howells in the days just after Christmas.

The entrance-hall fireplace featuring the brass fender that Twain gifted to Livy in 1875.

The first-floor guest room, known to the family as "the mahogany room," was reserved for special guests. Clemens' editor and friend, William Dean Howells, called it "the royal chamber."

"The work began many weeks before the holy day," Clara wrote. "Even so, there seemed always to be a rush at the end. A room we called the Mahogany room . . . was used for the storing of gifts and wrapping of packages. Mother had an almost German talent for thoroughness in any task she undertook. Yet in spite of her time saving system the labor of this annual job occupied many hours of her day for several weeks. If she could not be found anywhere in the house, one might guess that she was busy in the 'mahogany room,' writing lists of names and trying to determine the needs or wishes of each individual. Her energy and patience were incredible. Father did not approve of her doing so much long-sustained work, because he always worried about her health. But the Christmas complications seemed to increase rather than decrease as the years went on, and I remember his saying many times, after he lost his money and we left for Europe in order to live cheaply: 'I am glad, for one reason, that financial losses have struck us! Your mother will have to give up her infernal Christmas-suicide.' "

Clara and Jean shared the nursery. Susy, as the oldest child, had her own room. The wallpaper was an original pattern by illustrator Walter Crane and tells the nursery rhyme, "Ye Frog He Would A-Wooing Go"—or "Froggie Went A-Courtin' " as it is better known today—in words and pictures.

The house also had a room that was originally designed as Twain's study, which later became a play area and classroom for his daughters.

"Our school room provided memories never to be repeated," Clara wrote. "Snowstorms raging about many windows, against which a fire on the hearth cozily defended us."

They were educated by their mother and a governess, who taught them German, history, geography, and arithmetic, among other subjects. The Fischer upright piano now in the home is the same year and model as the one they were given for Christmas in 1880. The wall and ceiling decorations were done in 1879, by an Elmira, New York, decorator named Frederick Schweppe.

The house had been outfitted with speaking tubes that connected several of the private and public rooms with the kitchen, allowing the Clemens family to communicate with the house staff. There was one wall in the nursery, between Jean and Clara's twin brass beds, with such a speaking tube. Twain explained to the girls, in the days just before Christmas, that if they had forgotten to tell of a present they wanted, or had thought of a new present at the last minute, they could speak into the tube, and the bearded old St. Nick would be guaranteed to get the message.

"One of our cats, sarcastically called 'Apollinaris' was always dressed up in bows and invited in while we pinned up our stockings. He brought a certain balance of temperament with him that was very much needed. His Oriental calm kept us from bursting with excitement," Clara recalled years later.

"He is very fond of animals particularly cats," Susy stated in *Papa*, her biography of her father that she wrote when she was in her teens. "He had a dear little gray kitten once, that he named 'Lazy' (Papa always wears grey to match his gray hair and eyes) and he would carry him around on his shoulder, it was a mighty pretty sight! the gray cat sound asleep against Papa's gray coat and hair. The names that he has given our different cats, are really remarkably funny, they are namely Stray Kit, Abner, Motley, Fraeulein, Lazy, Buffalo Bill, Soapy Sall, Cleveland, Sour Mash, and Pestilence and Famine." The Clemenses also had a black cat named Satan, which gave birth to a similarly dark kitten that Sam respectively named Sin.

"A home without a cat—and a well-fed, well-petted and properly revered cat—may be a perfect home, perhaps, but how can it prove title?" Twain once wrote.

"When Christmas Eve arrived at last," Clara recalled, "we children hung up our stockings in the schoolroom next to our nursery, and did it with great ceremony. Mother always recited the trilling little poem, 'Twas the night before Christmas, when all through the house,' etc. Father sometimes dressed up as Santa Claus and, after running about a dimly lit room (we always turned the gas down low), trying to warm himself after the cold drive through the snow, he sat down and told some of his experiences on the way.

"His talk usually ended with something like this: 'As I often love those letters I receive, or get them mixed up, I may have confused your wishes, so that the stocking which should have bulged out with a donkey's head may be depressed by a hair ribbon. Therefore, I should like to gather up your thanks now, as you may not feel like giving me any after Christmas. Anyway, I shall be gone then.'

"We all squealed, 'Thank you, thank you, Santa Claus, for all the things we hope to like,' and after a short game of tag Father ran away to remove his cotton beard and red coat." Sam would then reappear as himself.

In 1875, Sam wrote the following letter to his then oldest daughter, Susy. She was four years old at the time, but the letter set the tone for the family's holidays for years to come.

Palace of St. Nicholas
In the Moon
Christmas Morning

MY DEAR SUSIE CLEMENS:

I have received and read all the letters which
you and your little sister have written me by
the hand of your mother and your nurses; I
have also read those which you little people
have written me with your own hands—for
although you did not use any characters
that are in grown peoples' alphabet, you
used the characters that all children in all
lands on earth and in the twinkling stars
use; and as all my subjects in the moon are
children and use no character but that, you
will easily understand that I can read your
and your baby sister's jagged and fantastic
marks without any trouble at all. But I had
trouble with those letters which you dictated through your mother and the nurses,
for I am a foreigner and cannot read English
writing well. You will find that I made no

mistakes about the things which you and the
baby ordered in your own letters—I went
down your chimney at midnight when you
were asleep and delivered them all myself—
and kissed both of you, too, because you
are good children, well trained, nice man-
nered, and about the most obedient little
people I ever saw. But in the letter which
you dictated there were some words which
I could not make out for certain, and one
or two small orders which I could not fill
because we ran out of stock. Our last lot
of kitchen furniture for dolls has just gone
to a very poor little child in the North Star
away up, in the cold country above the Big
Dipper. Your mama can show you that star
and you will say: "Little
Snow Flake," (for that is the
child's name) "I'm glad you
got that furniture, for you
need it more than I." That
is, you must write that, with
your own hand, and Snow

Flake will write you an answer. If you only spoke it she wouldn't hear you. Make your letter light and thin, for the distance is great and the postage very heavy.

There was a word or two in your mama's letter which I couldn't be certain of. I took it to be "a trunk full of doll's clothes." Is that it? I will call at your kitchen door about nine o'clock this morning to inquire. But I must not see anybody and I must not speak to anybody but you. When the kitchen doorbell rings, George must be blindfolded and sent to open the door. Then he must go back to the dining room or the china closet and take the cook with him. You must tell

George he must walk on tiptoe and not speak—otherwise he will die someday. Then you must go up to the nursery and stand on a chair or the nurse's bed and put your ear to the speaking tube that leads

down to the kitchen and when I whistle
through it you must speak in the tube and
say, "Welcome, Santa Claus!" Then I will
ask whether it was a trunk you ordered or
not. If you say it was, I shall ask you what
color you want the trunk to be. Your mama
will help you to name a nice color and then
you must tell me every single thing in detail
which you want the trunk to contain. Then
when I say "Good-by and a merry Christmas
to my little Susie Clemens," you must say
"Good-by, good old Santa Claus, I thank
you very much and please tell that little
Snow Flake I will look at her star tonight
and she must look down here—I will be
right in the west bay window; and every fine
night I will look at her star and say, 'I know
somebody up there and like her, too.' " Then
you must go down into the library and make
George close all the doors that open into
the main hall, and everybody must keep still
for a little while. I will go to the moon and
get those things and in a few minutes I will

come down the chimney that belongs to the fireplace that is in the hall—if it is a trunk you want—because I couldn't get such a thing as a trunk down the nursery chimney, you know.

People may talk if they want, until they hear my footsteps in the hall. Then you tell them to keep quiet a little while till I go back up the chimney. Maybe you will not hear my footsteps at all—so you may go now and then and peep through the dining-room doors, and by and by you will see that thing which you want, right under the piano in the drawing room—for I shall put it there. If I should leave any snow in the hall, you must tell George to sweep it into the fireplace, for I haven't time to do such things. George must not use a broom, but a rag—else he will die someday. You must watch George and not let him run into danger. If my boot should leave a stain on the marble, George

must not holystone it away. Leave it there always in memory of my visit; and whenever you look at it or show it to anybody you must let it remind you to be a good little girl. Whenever you are naughty and some-body points to that mark which your good old Santa Claus's boot made on the marble, what will you say, little sweetheart?

Good-by for a few minutes, till I come down to the world and ring the kitchen doorbell.

Your loving SANTA CLAUS
Whom people sometimes call
"The Man in the Moon"

Twain's "Man in the Moon" letter, and the boot print that "Santa" left behind, remained joyous reminders of the magic of the season throughout the Clemens family's years in their beloved Hartford home.

Clara wrote, "[M]y sisters and I were obliged to retire at an early hour every evening, not excepting

Christmas Eve. Therefore, by eight o'clock we were in bed, launched on a long night of wakefulness, while mother started on a night of work down in the 'mahogany room.' Two of us, Jean and I, slept in the nursery, and my eldest sister, Susy, occupied a little blue room adjoining. But, on Christmas Eve, Susy crept into my bed with me and we listened for the mysterious sounds that would betray the presence of fairies in the schoolroom.

"Ah, there they are! Rattling paper, subdued voices. A dull thud; something falls. I wonder what it is? If only it isn't broken! Oh, Susy, listen to that heavy thing they are dragging across the floor! What on earth can that be? I'll die if I can't find out soon. How many hours yet? If only we could sleep!

"As a matter of fact, we should have been tired enough to sleep, for the day before Christmas was always spent in a somewhat fatiguing way by my sisters and me. We drove around with the coachman while he delivered Christmas packages that went to the poor. Great baskets with the feet of turkeys protruding below blankets of flowers and fruits. Wrapped up in mufflers and snugly tucked in a fur robe, we children drove far out into the country in an open sleigh, tingling with delight at the sound of the bells. We absorbed all the beauty and charm of such a winter's day and could never get too much of the crisp air that was made to sparkle even more by the rapid pace the horses took over the soft, white ground.

"Finally, all became still in the schoolroom. The fairies must have gone. Not a sound. The forms left behind are motionless, speechless. Are they pretty? Are they useful? Shall we love them?

" 'Let's take one little peek through the door. With a tiny bit of light from the bathroom we might get an idea of the shapes without seeing anything,' Susy said.

"It didn't take me long to say, 'Yes.'

"Opening the door a few inches, and by means of a dim ray of light, we saw—'Oh, dear, shut the door quick! We must not look. That's wicked. What do you suppose that huge black thing can be? It seems to fill the room. Come, let's try to go to sleep.' Of course that was impossible.

"Eventually 6 A.M. came and we rang for the nurse to build a fire in the schoolroom and help us dress with as little washing as possible. And now the door opens wide! The great moment of revealed mysteries has arrived! Joy blazes supreme in that Christmas room, and natural instinct tells us to hold that first moment a little longer. Stop and gaze at the beauty of the unknown in undefined shapes and delicate tints.

"But at last each make a rush for her own table, scattering ribbons, papers, and ejaculations with vehement haste. Think of it. The big object seeming to fill the center of the room turns out to be a lovely upright piano. Can it be true? Once I had said to my parents: 'How wonderful it must be to be able to play on the piano! Do girls ever play?' And now here was a real live piano in front of my eyes and I was only six years old."

And down in the entrance hall, just beyond the brass fender Sam had given to Livy for Christmas, was Santa's footprint, painted black on the marble floor where he first set foot coming out of the chimney. For the entire time the Clemenses remained in the house, no matter the age of the girls, the foot-print remained, throughout the seasons, a constant reminder of Livy and Sam's enduring commitment to each other, and a reminder to their children of the return of Santa Claus.

"Father and Mother always rose very late on Christmas morning, having spent most of the night up. So we were well acquainted with our presents, and had even written several letters of thanks, before our parents appeared. They inspected their gifts, which were down in the drawing-room, and callers from the neighborhood would arrive," Clara wrote.

Dinner parties were very much part of the Clemens household, where they entertained numerous celebrities of the day, many of whom lived in Hartford and the surrounding areas.

"When dinner parties were given, Susy and I used to sit on the stairs and listen to the broken bits of conversation coming from the dining room," Clara wrote. "We got into this habit because we used to hear so many peals of laughter in the distance that we would run to discover the cause of the mirth. Almost always, it turned out that Father was telling a funny story. Now, it happened that a few times

Father had told the same story on various occasions when the guests were dining at the house and we had calculated that each time the meal was about half over. So we used to announce to one another, 'Father is telling the beggar story; they must have reached the meat course.' When he discovered his children were taking their turn at having jokes about him, he laughed as much as if he had been very witty."

"I am never more tickled than when I laugh at myself," Twain once remarked.

"Father, however, always drew a sigh of relief when the holidays were over," Clara fondly recalled. "The reason was that they included social festivities that were sometimes a burden to him, particularly if he happened to be in the mood of writing; and this mood, he was want to declare, always attacked him when some 'mentally dead people brought their corpses with them for a long visit.' "

1909

The Last Christmas

Stormfield was festooned with garlands and flowers and seasonal decorations. Evergreen boughs and poinsettias framed all the rooms downstairs, yet the house was quiet this Christmas Eve morning in 1909. The snow swirled and the gray skies delivered a howling wind. Sam Clemens sat in a chair, a blanket around him. He could not keep warm. He was silent, thinking.

He harkened back to the day he last walked into the old house in Hartford. It was in March of 1895. He was back in America, alone, and decided to visit the house while traveling. The family had moved to Europe four years earlier, and would maintain ownership of the house until 1903, but never lived there again as a family after departing for the Continent. Upon that March visit, he wrote to Livy, ". . . [A]s soon as I entered this front door I was seized with a furious desire to have us all in the house again & right away, & never go outside the grounds any more forever. . . ." Twain wrote of the "perfect taste of this ground floor, with its delicious dream of harmonious color, & its all-pervading spirit of peace

and serenity and deep contentment. . . . It is the loveliest home that ever was."

Could it be Susy had been gone now thirteen years?

During the summer of 1896, Sam completed an around-the-world speaking tour meant to replenish his bank account that was nearly exhausted due to lavish spending and bad investments. While Sam, Livy, and Clara traveled abroad to Europe, Susy decided to stay home, and Jean with her. While Sam and Livy were away, Susy had grown ill. Sam cursed himself and his mistakes, and apologized to Livy again and again, insisting that Suzy's illness was his fault.

"The last thirteen days of Susy's life were spent in our own house in Hartford, the home of her childhood and always the dearest place in the earth to her," Clemens wrote.

"On August 15 the doctor diagnosed Susy's illness as spinal meningitis. That evening, she ate for the last time," wrote Twain biographer Charles Neider. In a letter Jean wrote to Sam, she described in detail Susy's last few days.

"The next morning, a Sunday, she walked about in pain and delirium . . . rummaging in her closet, she came across a gown she had once seen her mother wear. She thought it was her dead mother, and kissing it, began to cry." In her last hours, she wrote more than a thousand words of delirious stream-of-consciousness scribbling, and ran to the window, chanting, "Up go the trolley cars for Mark Twain's daughter. Down go the trolley cars for Mark Twain's daughter."

Susy died on August 18th, 1896. Clara and her mother were onboard ship when the news came. A steward asked Clara to visit the captain. "He handed me a newspaper with great headlines: 'Mark Twain's eldest daughter dies of spinal meningitis.' . . . [The] world stood still. All sounds and movement ceased. Susy was dead. How could I tell mother? I went to her stateroom. Nothing was said. A deadly pallor spread over her face and then came a bursting cry. 'I don't believe it!' And we never did believe it."

Clemens, for his part, was alone still in a house in England. "I was standing in our dining room thinking of nothing in particular, when a cablegram was put into my hand. It said, 'Susy was peacefully released today.' It is one of the mysteries of our nature that a man, all unprepared, can receive a thunder-stroke like that and live. . . . On the 23rd her mother and sisters saw her laid to rest—she that had been our wonder and our worship." And, he wrote to a friend, "Our loss is bitter, bitter, bitter. Then what must it be to my wife. It would bankrupt all vocabularies of all the languages to put it into words."

"After Susy's death in 1896 it was Olivia who refused to live in the Hartford home where they had raised their children," Rebecca Floyd wrote. "The family's grief was intensified by Jean's struggle with epilepsy. In her 1931 memoir *My Father: Mark Twain*, Clara reminisced that no one in the family smiled for a long time. In the years after Susy's death, the family lived a somewhat nomadic existence, mostly in Europe. The perpetual travel and Jean's need for ongoing care took its toll on Olivia's health. Clemens described it as 'five years of constant anxiety, and periodical shocks and frights.' In August 1902, Olivia suffered what was probably a heart attack. She had chest pain and difficulty breathing. Her health continued to deteriorate.

"Late in 1903 the family decided to travel to Florence, Italy, where they thought the pleasant climate would improve Olivia's health. Sam was kept separate from her for much of her last months. She was supposed to be kept quiet and unexcited, so he would send little love notes to her twice a day. He would break the rules and make brief visits to sit with her and give her kisses. Clara and their longtime maid, Katy Leary, spent the most time with Livy. Clara would make sure that no news of Jean's illness was shared with their mother, to keep her from worrying. Jean, in turn, was not allowed to hear about her mother's failing health. Clara suffered terribly as this intermediary.

"Livy died on June 5, 1904. Her death would leave a hole in the family that neither of his daughters or friends could fill. In their memoirs and letters, Clara, Katy—and particularly the stricken Sam Clemens himself—commented on their inability to take part in everyday life, travel, and writing after Livy's death."

"She was my life, and she is gone; she was my riches, and now I am a pauper. . . . She was the most beautiful spirit, and the highest and the noblest I have ever known. And now she is dead," lamented the broken Twain.

Later in life, Clemens expressed regret that he had not spent more time with his children, writing, "We are always too busy for our children; we never give them the time nor the interest they deserve. We lavish gifts upon them; but the most precious gift—our personal association, which means so much to them—we give grudgingly and throw it away on those who care for it so little. But we are repaid for it at last. There comes a time when we want their company and their interest. We want it more than anything in the world, and we are likely to be starved for it, just as they were starved so long ago."

In October of 1909, Clara had married at the grand Italianate villa of Stormfield. The house had been festooned with flowers and abuzz with people. It had reminded Sam of the old days. He was telling stories and entertaining people, and his daughter was happy. Clara and Ossip Gabrilowitsch (her husband) were now living in London.

Jean had been in and out of sanitariums most of her adult life, but with Susy and Livy gone, and Clara married and living in London, Sam wanted to spend more time with his youngest daughter, whom he admitted he did not know well enough. He arranged for her return to Stormfield in April of 1909 to serve as his caretaker and secretary.

She ran the house, took care of his correspondence, and ran a small farm of her own in a field near Stormfield, which she often inspected on horseback in the mornings. She was competent if not sometimes hardheaded, a trait inherited from her father. After years of being taken care of as an invalid, it was now she taking care of her frail and irascible father.

Twain and his youngest daughter, Jean.

Jean tended to her farm on horseback daily.

"He had feared for many months that she might be stricken while on horseback, far away on the lonely country roads, and that she might be mangled beneath the horse's hoofs. He had many warnings that his daughter might be stricken down. Less than a month ago she suffered a violent attack of epilepsy, and for several years she had been under the constant care of an attendant. For several months Miss Clemens was in a sanitarium, but in April last had come to Stormfield in order to be her father's housekeeper and to help him in his literary work as his secretary," the *New York Times* had reported on Christmas Eve, 1909.

"Miss Clemens herself had no thought of death . . . she invited one of her girl friends in New York to come to Stormfield to spend the holidays and elaborate plans had been made for a jolly Christmas. This friend had been instructed to come today on the Pittsfield express, and Mark Twain had arranged with the New York, New Haven & Hartford officials to have the train stop at Redding. . . ." continued the *Times* article.

Twain had celebrated his seventy-fourth birthday in Bermuda. He was having a wonderful time there, and had written his daughter Clara in London: "Never in my life before, perhaps, have I had such a strong sense of being severed from the world, & all the bridges swept away."

Twain had joked that he left for Bermuda to escape Thanksgiving. He had thought at one point to stay in Bermuda through the rest of the holidays, but was entreated by his youngest daughter to return to the States for a more traditional Christmas. With the holidays approaching, Jean did her best to continue the seasonal traditions created by her mother, which she and her father had experienced in years past. Wreaths on the door. Garlands in the house. The fresh scent of the boughs filling the villa. It was a Twain Christmas come again.

Jean and a passel of reporters greeted Twain as he disembarked in New York City on December 20, 1909. "Miss Clemens went to New York with her maid to meet her father on his arrival from Bermuda. She took advantage of her presence in town to buy several Christmas presents for her friends. Some of these she sent by mail . . ." reported the *New York Times*.

"He was not in the jovial mood so apparent on his return from the Bermudas last year with his close friends, the late Mr. H. H. Rogers. Whenever Mr. Clemens met the reporters he always had something humorous up his sleeve to drop casually when an interview was under way. It was different yesterday," reported the *New York Tribune* the following day. "The reporters clutched at straws to bring forth some droll remark."

The weather was cold and he was uncomfortable.

"When I got down to Bermuda, that pain in the breast left me; now, on my return, I have got it again," he complained to the throng. "I am through with work for this life and this world."

When one reporter asked if he would lecture on behalf of women's rights, he scoffed, "The state of my health will not permit it. The fact is that I am through with work. I have no new books in contemplation."

In the papers, there had been a rumor that Twain had died. He was content to let the rumor drift, but Jean pleaded with him: What if Clara were to read the news in London? How would she react? Twain was moved by this argument, and released a statement to the press.

THE NEW YORK TIMES, DECEMBER 24, 1909
TWAIN'S MERRY CHRISTMAS.

Humorist Says He Would Not Think of Dying at His Time of Life.

REDDING, Conn., Dec. 23. - Mark Twain today gave out the following statement as a result of various reports concerning his condition of health, following his recent return from Bermuda:

"I hear the newspapers say I am dying.
The charge is not true. I would not do such
a thing at my time of life. I am behaving
as good as I can. Merry Christmas to
everybody!

"MARK TWAIN"

His acquiescence had pleased Jean immeasurably. "My daughter was trimming the tree yesterday and I was helping her," Twain later told the *New York Times*. "She was so anxious that the lads and lassies of the neighborhood should have a tree, so we brought this one in and began to trim it for them. . . . [They] were to have trooped in to see the tree and to get presents from it."

The rest of the story is straight from Twain's own hand:

Last night Jean, all flushed with splendid health, and I the same, from the wholesome effects of my Bermuda holiday, strolled hand in hand from the dinner-table and sat down in the library and chatted, and planned, and discussed, cheerily and happily (and how unsuspectingly!)—until nine—which is late for us—then went upstairs, Jean's friendly German dog following. At my door Jean said, "I can't kiss you good night, father: I have a cold, and you could catch it." I bent and kissed her hand. She was moved—I saw it in her eyes—and she impulsively kissed my hand in return. Then with the usual gay "Sleep well, dear!" from both, we parted.

At half past seven this morning I woke, and heard voices outside my door. I said to myself, "Jean is starting on her usual horseback flight to the station for the mail." Then Katy entered, stood quaking and gasping at my bed-side a moment, then found her tongue:

"MISS JEAN IS DEAD!"

Possibly I know now what the soldier feels when a bullet crashes through his heart.

In her bathroom there she lay, the fair young creature, stretched upon the floor and covered with a sheet. And looking so placid, so natural, and as if asleep. We knew what had happened. She was an epileptic: she had been seized with a convulsion and heart failure in her bath. The doctor had to come several miles. His efforts, like our previous ones, failed to bring her back to life.

It is noon, now. How lovable she looks, how sweet and how tranquil! It is a noble face, and full of dignity; and that was a good heart that lies there so still.

In England, thirteen years ago, my wife and I were stabbed to the heart with a cablegram which said, "Susy was mercifully released today." I had to send a like shot to Clara, in Berlin, this morning. With the peremptory addition, "You must not come home." Clara and her husband sailed from here on the 11th of this month. How will Clara bear it? Jean, from her babyhood, was a worshiper of Clara.

Four days ago I came back from a month's holiday in Bermuda in perfected health; but by some accident the reporters failed to perceive this. Day before yesterday, letters and telegrams began to arrive from friends and strangers which indicated that I was supposed to be dangerously ill. Yesterday Jean begged me to explain my case through the Associated Press. I said it was not important enough; but she was distressed and said I must think of Clara. Clara would see the report in the German papers, and as she had been nursing her husband day and night for four months and was worn out and feeble, the shock might be disastrous. There was reason in that; so I sent a humorous paragraph by telephone to the Associated Press denying the "charge" that I was "dying," and saying "I would not do such a thing at my time of life."

Jean was a little troubled, and did not like to see me treat the matter so lightly; but I said it was best to treat it so, for there was nothing serious about it. This morning I sent the sorrowful facts of this day's irremediable disaster to the Associated Press. Will both appear in this evening's papers?—the one so blithe, the other so tragic?

I lost Susy thirteen years ago; I lost her mother—her incomparable mother!—five and a half years ago; Clara has gone away to live in Europe; and now I have lost Jean. How poor I am, who was once so rich! Seven months ago Mr. Roger died—one of the best friends I ever had, and the nearest perfect, as man and gentleman, I have yet met among my race; within the last six weeks Gilder has passed away, and Laffan—old, old friends of mine. Jean lies yonder, I sit here; we are strangers under our own roof; we kissed hands good-by at this door last night—and it was forever, we never suspecting it. She lies there, and I sit here—writing, busying myself, to keep my heart from breaking. How dazzlingly the sunshine is flooding the hills around! It is like a mockery.

Seventy-four years ago twenty-four days ago. Seventy-four years old yesterday. Who can estimate my age today?

I have looked upon her again. I wonder I can bear it. She looks just as her mother looked when she lay dead in that Florentine villa so long ago. The sweet placidity of death! it is more beautiful than sleep.

I saw her mother buried. I said I would never endure that horror again; that I would never again look into the grave of any one dear to me. I have kept to that. They will take Jean from this house tomorrow, and bear her to Elmira, New York, where lie those of us that have been released, but I shall not follow.

Jean was on the dock when the ship came in, only four days ago. She was at the door, beaming a welcome, when I reached this house the next evening. We played cards, and she tried to teach me a new game called "Mark Twain." We sat chatting cheerily in the library last night, and she wouldn't let me look into the loggia, where she was making Christmas preparations. She said she would finish them in the morning, and then her little French friend would arrive from New York—the surprise would follow; the surprise she had been working over for days. While she was out for a moment I disloyally stole a look. The loggia floor was clothed with rugs and furnished with chairs and sofas; and the uncompleted surprise was there: in the form of a Christmas tree that was drenched with silver film in a most wonderful way; and on a table was prodigal profusion of bright things which she was going to hang upon it today. What desecrating hand will ever banish that eloquent unfinished surprise from that place? Not mine, surely. All these little matters have happened in the last four days. "Little." Yes—THEN. But not now. Nothing she said or thought or did is little now. And all the lavish humor!—what is become of it? It is pathos, now. Pathos, and the thought of it brings tears.

All these little things happened such a few hours ago—and now she lies yonder. Lies yonder, and cares for nothing any more. Strange—marvelous—incredible! I have had this experience before; but it would still be incredible if I had had it a thousand times.

"MISS JEAN IS DEAD!"

That is what Katy said. When I heard the door open behind the bed's head without a preliminary knock, I supposed it was Jean coming to kiss me good morning, she being the only person who was used to entering without formalities.

And so—

I have been to Jean's parlor. Such a turmoil of Christmas presents for servants and friends! They are everywhere; tables, chairs, sofas, the floor—everything is occupied, and over-occupied. It is many and many a year since I have seen the like. In that ancient day Mrs. Clemens and I used to slip softly into the nursery at midnight on Christmas Eve and look the array of presents over. The children were little then. And now here is Jean's parlor looking just as that nursery used to look. The presents are not labeled—the hands are forever idle that would have labeled them today. Jean's mother always worked herself down with her Christmas preparations. Jean did the same yesterday and the preceding days, and the fatigue has cost her

her life. The fatigue caused the convulsion that attacked her this morning. She had had no attack for months.

Jean was so full of life and energy that she was constantly is danger of overtaxing her strength. Every morning she was in the saddle by half past seven, and off to the station for her mail. She examined the letters and I distributed them: some to her, some to Mr. Paine, the others to the stenographer and myself. She dispatched her share and then mounted her horse again and went around superintending her farm and her poultry the rest of the day. Sometimes she played billiards with me after dinner, but she was usually too tired to play, and went early to bed.

Yesterday afternoon I told her about some plans I had been devising while absent in Bermuda, to lighten her burdens. We would get a housekeeper; also we would put her share of the secretary-work into Mr. Paine's hands.

No—she wasn't willing. She had been making plans herself. The matter ended in a compromise, I submitted. I always did. She wouldn't audit the bills and let Paine fill out the checks—she would continue to attend to that herself. Also, she would continue to be housekeeper, and let Katy assist. Also, she would continue to answer the letters of personal friends for me. Such was the compromise. Both of us called it by that name, though I was not able to see where my formidable change had been made.

However, Jean was pleased, and that was sufficient for me. She was proud of being my secretary, and I was never able to persuade her to give up any part of her share in that unlovely work.

In the talk last night I said I found everything going so smoothly that if she were willing I would go back to Bermuda in February and get blessedly out of the clash and turmoil again for another month. She was urgent that I should do it, and said that if I would put off the trip until March she would take Katy and go with me. We struck hands upon that, and said it was settled. I had a mind to write to Bermuda by tomorrow's ship and secure a furnished house and servants. I meant to write the letter this morning. But it will never be written, now.

For she lies yonder, and before her is another journey than that.

Night is closing down; the rim of the sun barely shows above the sky-line of the hills.

I have been looking at that face again that was growing dearer and dearer to me every day. I was getting acquainted with Jean in these last nine months. She had been long an exile from home when she came to us three-quarters of a year ago. She had been shut up in sanitariums, many miles from us. How eloquent glad and grateful she was to cross her father's threshold again!

Would I bring her back to life if I could do it? I would not. If a word would do it, I would beg for strength to withhold the word. And I would have the strength; I am sure of it. In her loss I am almost bankrupt, and my life is a bitterness, but I am content: for she has been enriched with the most precious of all gifts—that gift which makes all other gifts mean and poor—death. I have never wanted any released friend of mine restored to life since I reached manhood. I felt in this way when Susy passed away; and later my wife, and later Mr. Rogers. When Clara met me at the station in New York and told me Mr. Rogers had died suddenly that morning, my thought was, Oh, favorite of fortune—fortunate all his long and lovely life—fortunate to his latest moment! The reporters said there were tears of sorrow in my eyes. True—but they were for ME, not for him. He had suffered no loss. All the fortunes he had ever made before were poverty compared with this one.

Why did I build this house, two years ago? To shelter this vast emptiness? How foolish I was! But I shall stay in it. The spirits of the dead hallow a house, for me. It was not so with other members of the family. Susy died in the house we built in Hartford. Mrs. Clemens would never enter it again. But it made the house dearer to me. I have entered it once since, when it was tenantless and silent and forlorn, but to me it was a holy place and beautiful. It seemed to me that the spirits of the dead were all about me, and would speak to me and welcome me if they could: Livy, and Susy, and George, and Henry Robinson, and Charles Dudley Warner. How good and kind they were, and how lovable their lives! In fancy I could see them all again, I could call the children back and hear them romp again with George—that peerless black ex-slave and children's idol who came one day—a flitting stranger—to wash windows, and stayed eighteen years. Until he died. Clara and Jean would never enter again the New York hotel which their mother had frequented in earlier days. They could not bear it. But I shall stay in this house. It is dearer to me tonight than ever it was before. Jean's spirit will make it beautiful for me always. Her lonely and tragic death—but I will not think of that now.

Jean's mother always devoted two or three weeks to Christmas shopping, and was always physically exhausted when Christmas Eve came. Jean was her very own child—she wore herself out present- hunting in New York these latter days. Paine has just found on her desk a long list of names—fifty, he thinks—people to whom she sent presents last night. Apparently she forgot no one. And Katy found there a roll of bank-notes, for the servants.

Her dog has been wandering about the grounds today, comradeless and forlorn. I have seen him from the windows. She got him from Germany. He has tall ears and looks exactly like a wolf. He was educated in Germany, and knows no language but the German. Jean gave him no orders save in that tongue. And so when the burglar-alarm made a fierce clamor at midnight a fortnight ago, the butler, who is French and knows no German, tried in vain to interest the dog in the supposed burglar. Jean wrote me, to Bermuda, about the incident. It was the last letter I was ever to receive from her bright head and her competent hand. The dog will not be neglected.

There was never a kinder heart than Jean's. From her childhood up she always spent the most of her allowance on charities of one kind or another. After she became secretary and had her income doubled she spent her money upon these things with a free hand. Mine too, I am glad and grateful to say.

She was a loyal friend to all animals, and she loved them all, birds, beasts, and everything—even snakes—an inheritance from me. She knew all the birds; she was high up in that lore. She became a member of various humane societies when she was still a little girl—both here and abroad—and she remained an active member to the last. She founded two or three societies for the protection of animals, here and in Europe.

She was an embarrassing secretary, for she fished my correspondence out of the waste-basket and answered the letters. She thought all letters deserved the courtesy of an answer. Her mother brought her up in that kindly error.

She could write a good letter, and was swift with her pen. She had but an indifferent ear music, but her tongue took to languages with an easy facility. She never allowed her Italian, French, and German to get rusty through neglect.

The telegrams of sympathy are flowing in, from far and wide, now, just as they did in Italy five years and a half ago, when this child's mother laid down her blameless life. They cannot heal the hurt, but they take away some of the pain. When Jean and I kissed hands and parted at my door last, how little did we imagine that in twenty-two hours the telegraph would be bringing words like these:

"From the bottom of our hearts we send out sympathy, dearest of friends."

For many and many a day to come, wherever I go in this house, remembrancers of Jean will mutely speak to me of her. Who can count the number of them?

She was in exile two years with the hope of healing her malady—epilepsy. There are no words to express how grateful I am that she did not meet her fate in the hands of strangers, but in the loving shelter of her own home.

"MISS JEAN IS DEAD!"

It is true. Jean is dead.

A month ago I was writing bubbling and hilarious articles for magazines yet to appear, and now I am writing—this.

CHRISTMAS DAY. NOON.—Last night I went to Jean's room at intervals, and turned back the sheet and looked at the peaceful face, and kissed the cold brow, and remembered that heartbreaking night in Florence so long ago, in that cavernous and silent vast villa, when I crept downstairs so many times, and turned back a sheet and looked at a face just like this one—Jean's mother's face—and kissed a brow that was just like this one. And last night I saw again what I had seen then—that strange and lovely miracle—the sweet, soft contours of early maidenhood restored by the gracious hand of death! When Jean's mother lay dead, all trace of care, and trouble, and suffering, and the corroding years had vanished out of the face, and I was looking again upon it as

I had known and worshipped it in its young bloom and beauty a whole generation before.

About three in the morning, while wandering about the house in the deep silences, as one does in times like these, when there is a dumb sense that something has been lost that will never be found again, yet must be sought, if only for the employment the useless seeking gives, I came upon Jean's dog in the hall downstairs, and noted that he did not spring to greet me, according to his hospitable habit, but came slow and sorrowfully; also I remembered that he had not visited Jean's apartment since the tragedy. Poor fellow, did he know? I think so. Always when Jean was abroad in the open he was with her; always when she was in the house he was with her, in the night as well as in the day. Her parlor was his bedroom. Whenever I happened upon him on the ground floor he always followed me about, and when I went upstairs he went too—in a tumultuous gallop. But now it was different: after patting him a little I went to the library—he remained behind; when I went upstairs he did not follow me, save with his wistful eyes. He has wonderful eyes—big, and kind, and eloquent. He can talk with them. He is a beautiful creature, and is of the breed of the New York police-dogs. I do not like dogs, because they bark when there is no occasion for it; but I have liked this one from the beginning, because he belonged to Jean, and because he never barks except when there is occasion—which is not oftener than twice a week.

In my wanderings I visited Jean's parlor. On a shelf I found a pile of my books, and I knew what it meant. She was waiting for me to come home from Bermuda and autograph them, then she would send them away. If I only knew whom she intended them for! But I shall never know. I will keep them. Her hand has touched them—it is an accolade—they are noble, now.

And in a closet she had hidden a surprise for me—a thing I have often wished I owned: a noble big globe. I couldn't see it for the tears. She will never know the pride I take in it, and the pleasure. Today the mails are full of loving remembrances for her: full of those old, old kind words she loved so well, "Merry Christmas to Jean!" If she could only have lived one day longer!

At last she ran out of money, and would not use mine. So she sent to one of those New York homes for poor girls all the clothes she could spare—and more, most likely.

CHRISTMAS NIGHT.—This afternoon they took her away from her room. As soon as I might, I went down to the library, and there she lay, in her coffin, dressed in exactly the same clothes she wore when she stood at the other end of the same room on the 6th of October last, as Clara's chief bridesmaid. Her face was radiant with happy excitement then; it was the same face now, with the dignity of death and the peace of God upon it.

They told me the first mourner to come was the dog. He came uninvited, and stood up on his hind legs and rested his fore paws upon the trestle, and took a last long look at the face that was so dear to him, then went his way as silently as he had come. HE KNOWS.

At mid-afternoon it began to snow. The pity of it—that Jean could not see it! She so loved the snow.

The snow continued to fall. At six o'clock the hearse drew up to the door to bear away its pathetic burden. As they lifted the casket, Paine began playing on the orchestrelle Schubert's "Impromptu," which was Jean's favorite. Then he played the Intermezzo; that was for Susy; then he played the Largo; that was for their mother. He did this at my request. Elsewhere in my Autobiography I have told how the Intermezzo and the Largo came to be associated in my heart with Susy and Livy in their last hours in this life.

From my windows I saw the hearse and the carriages wind along the road and gradually grow vague and spectral in the falling snow, and presently disappear. Jean was gone out of my life, and would not come back any more. Jervis, the cousin she had played with when they were babies together—he and her beloved old Katy—were conducting her to her distant childhood home, where she will lie by her mother's side once more, in the company of Susy and Langdon.

DECEMBER 26TH. The dog came to see me at eight o'clock this morning. He was very affectionate, poor orphan! My room will be his quarters hereafter.

The storm raged all night. It has raged all the morning. The snow drives across the landscape in vast clouds, superb, sublime—and Jean not here to see.

2:30 P.M.—It is the time appointed. The funeral has begun. Four hundred miles away, but I can see it all, just as if I were there. The scene is the library in the Langdon homestead. Jean's coffin stands where her mother and I stood, forty years ago, and were married; and where Susy's coffin stood thirteen years ago; where her mother's stood five years and a half ago; and where mine will stand after a little time.

FIVE O'CLOCK.—It is all over.

When Clara went away two weeks ago to live in Europe, it was hard, but I could bear it, for I had Jean left. I said WE would be a family. We said we would be close comrades and happy—just we two. That fair dream was in my mind when Jean met me at the steamer last Monday; it was in my mind when she received me at the door last Tuesday evening. We were together; WE WERE A FAMILY! the dream had come true—oh, precisely true, contentedly, true, satisfyingly true! and remained true two whole days.

And now? Now Jean is in her grave!

In the grave—if I can believe it. God rest her sweet spirit!

To Mrs. Gabrilowitsch, in Europe:

REDDING, CONN.,

Dec. 29, '09.

O, Clara, Clara dear, I am so glad she is out
of it and safe—safe! I am not melancholy;
I shall never be melancholy again, I think.
You see, I was in such distress when I came
to realize that you were gone far away and
no one stood between her and danger but
me—and I could die at any moment, and
then—oh then what would become of her!
For she was willful, you know, and would
not have been governable.

You can't imagine what a darling she was, that last two or three days; and how fine, and good, and sweet, and noble—and joyful, thank Heaven!—and how intellectually brilliant. I had never been acquainted with Jean before. I recognized that.

But I mustn't try to write about her—I can't. I have already poured my heart out with the pen, recording that last day or two.

I will send you that—and you must let no one but Ossip read it.

Good-bye.

I love you so!

And Ossip.

FATHER.

Four months later, on April 21, 1910, he was with Jean.

The Gift

Today, more than fifty thousand people walk through the halls of Mark Twain's home each year, thrilled to see where the great literary humorist lived, ate and slept, and created many of literature's greatest characters and stories. Mark Twain only visited the Hartford house one more time in his life after Susy's death. For him, the house was filled with happy memories, and many ghosts. Since Twain sold the property in 1903, it has passed through many hands, having been a library, a private school, and an apartment building before it was eventually restored to its former glory, and opened to the public in 1974.

But what might have been meant only for his family, turns out to have been the most lasting of all his gifts.

At Christmas time, the house is decked out as it was in the old days, with wreaths and garlands outside, and Christmas trees and poinsettias inside.

Visitors walk up the path to the giant red brick house that Livy designed and built. And they pass through the front door, and come into full view of the entrance hall.

And there on the floor, in front of the fireplace, is the brass fender that Twain made a Christmas present of to Livy.

And there, just beyond it, is the black shadow of Santa's footprint, still marking the hearth of the house in Hartford to this day.

Acknowledgements

Any author of such an effort owes a great debt of gratitude to those who went before him. Several writers' works have proved invaluable, including Albert Bigelow Paine, Ron Powers, Justin Kaplan, Fred Kaplan, Charles Neider, William Dean Howells, Michael Shelden, and of course Twain's children Clara Clemens and Susy Clemens, and, the many historians who wrote about Twain throughout the years.

Of course, I pored over more than five hundred original sources, including some one-thousand letters and interviews with Twain, his children, their household members, and biographies of friends and literary partners, searching for hints of Christmas here and there to weave into this story.

As ever, I owe a debt of special thanks in all of my professional endeavors to Gilbert King for his ear, opinions, advice, general good cheer, and encouragement. Others who also cheered me on were Michael Fragnito and Caitlin Friedman, among others.

I would, of course, like to thank John Whalen of Cider Mill Press Book Publishers, who helped make this book a reality. Were it not for his excitement, enthusiasm, and faith in me, I might have given up under the weight of this massive project. I also owe a huge debt of gratitude to editors Kate Cathey, Suzanne Brown, and Greg Jones who helped mold a rather large manuscript into readable shape, and to Whitney Cookman and Alicia Freile for the wonderful jacket and interior design, respectively. And special thanks to Patti Philippon and Beatrice Fox Auerbach, Chief Curator of the Mark Twain House, and to the many guides who ferried me and my family through the Clemens house countless times.

Special thanks to Cindy Lovell, Executive Director at the Mark Twain House & Museum, for her help and advice.

I would like to thank my sons, Dylan and Dawson, whom I have taken too much time away from in order to pursue not only this work, but also my other professional aspirations. I have tried to attend as many of their basketball, baseball, and track events as possible, but there is no replacement for a catch or an ice-cream cone, many of which were robbed by my other pursuits. I vow to them to spend more time hanging out and less time working.

Notes

PART ONE: 1908—THE ELEPHANT IN THE ROOM

Robert Joseph Collier was. . . N/A, "R. J. Collier Dies at Dinner Table," *The New York Times*, November 9, 1918

"The news created a disturbance in. . ." Paine, Albert Bigelow, *Mark Twain: A Biography, 1835-1910*, Project Gutenberg, 2006

"Twain bought the expansive property. . ." Karas, Alyssa, "An Exclusive Peek of Stormfield, Twain's Last Home," November 14, 2011, http://travelingwithtwain.org/2011/11/14/redding-ct/an-exclusive-peek-of-stormfield-twains-last-home/

"On the 18th of June, 1908. . ." Colley, Brent M., "Mark Twain's Redding, Connecticut Home: Stormfield," http://www.historyofredding.com/

HRtwainstormfield.htm

"Waiting for us at the Redding station. . ." Colley,
    "Mark Twain's Redding, Connecticut Home:
    Stormfield," http://www.historyofredding.com/
    HRtwainstormfield.htm

"I was never in this beautiful region. . ." Twain,
    Mark, Letter to Dorothy Quick, June 19, 1908

"Won't you and Mrs. Howells and. . ." Twain, Mark,
    Letter to William Dean Howells, August 12, 1908

"Not that he was really old. . ." Paine, *Mark Twain:
    A Biography, 1835-1910*, Project Gutenberg, 2006

"While living at Stormfield. . ." Karas, "An
    Exclusive Peek of Stormfield, Twain's
    Last Home," November 14, 2011, http://
    travelingwithtwain.org/2011/11/14/redding-ct/an-
    exclusive-peek-of-stormfield-twains-last-home/

"Mr. Lounsbury and Deputy Sheriff. . ." N/A,
    "Burglars Invade Mark Twain Villa," *The New
    York Times*, September 19, 1908

"Notice. To the Next Burglar. . . ." N/A, "Burglars
    Invade Mark Twain Villa," *The New York Times*,
    September 19, 1908

"To send an elephant in a trance. . ." Twain, Mark,

Letter to Joseph P. Collier

PART TWO: 1875—SANTA'S FOOTPRINT

"The approach of Christmas brings. . ." Twain,
    Mark, *Following the Equator*

"Samuel Clemens had spent much. . ." Powers, Ron,
    Mark Twain: A Life, Free Press, New York, NY,
    2005, p. 381

"Question: If a Congress of Presbyterians. . ."
    Powers, p. 380

"While traveling Clemens met his. . ." Philippon,
    Patti; Auerbach, Beatrice Fox, "A Home—& The
    Word Never Had So Much Meaning Before,"
    http://www.marktwainhouse.org/house/history.
    php

"In 1871, Sam moved his family. . ." Philippon
    and Auerbach, "A Home—& The Word Never
    Had So Much Meaning Before," http://www.
    marktwainhouse.org/house/history.php

"Livy had strong opinions about. . ." Philippon
    and Auerbach, "A Home—& The Word
    Never Had So Much Meaning Before,"
    http://www.marktwainhouse.org/house/history.

php

There was also a servant's wing. . . Sterner, Daniel,
A *Guide to Historic Hartford*, Connecticut,
The History Press, 2012

Livy's family was well-to-do. . . Floyd, Rebecca,
"Olivia 'Livy' Langdon Clemens," http://www.
marktwainhouse.org/man/olivia_langdon_
clemens.php

"[Livy] is so much more thoughtful. . ." Floyd,
"Olivia 'Livy' Langdon Clemens," http://www.
marktwainhouse.org/man/olivia_langdon_
clemens.php

"Sam Clemens entered Olivia's life. . ." Floyd,
"Olivia 'Livy' Langdon Clemens," http://www.
marktwainhouse.org/man/olivia_langdon_
clemens.php

"I feel ashamed of my idleness. . ." Twain, Mark,
Letter to Jane Clemens and family, June 4, 1868

"To Mrs. Clemens on her Thirtieth Birthday. . ."
Twain, Mark, Letter to Olivia Langdon Clemens,
November 27, 1875

"Mother wore very beautiful dresses. . ." Clemens,
Clara, *My Father, Mark Twain*, Harper & Brothers

Publishers, NY, 1931, p. 3

"When my thoughts return to. . ." Clemens,
Clara, p. 3

"A toboggan slide had to be arranged. . ." Clemens,
Clara, p. 4-5

"Father also taught us to skate. . ." Clemens,
Clara, p. 44

"They say God made man in his own effigy. . ."
Fisher, Henry, *Abroad with Mark Twain
and Eugene Field*, West Richard, 1922,
p. 212

"Smoke? I always smoke from 3 till 5 Sunday. . ."
Twain, Mark, Letter to Reverend Twichell,
December 19, 1870

"He smokes a great deal almost incessantly. . ."
Clemens, Susy, *Papa*, Doubleday & Co., Garden
City, NY, 1985, p. 89

The billiard room served as Mark Twain's office.
. . Floyd, Rebecca, "Room by Room: A Home
Brought to Life," http://www.marktwainhouse.
org/house/room_in_the_house.php

"Every Friday evening, or oftener. . ." Mark Twain
Library and Memorial Commission, *Mark Twain*

In Hartford, 1958, p. 24-25

"I wonder why a man should prefer. . ." Paine, *Mark Twain: A Biography, 1835-1910*, Project Gutenberg, 2006

"Mr. Clemens spent most of his time up. . ." Mark Twain Library and Memorial Commission, *Mark Twain in Hartford*, 1958, p. 24-25

"This is a most amusing game. . ." Es, Karl, "Shooting Pool with Mark Twain," *Sports Illustrated*, February 26, 1962

"Mark Twain always had a genuine passion. . ." Paine, *Mark Twain: A Biography, 1835-1910*, Project Gutenberg, 2006

"Both father and mother. . ." Clemens, Clara, p. 35

"I shall never forget the royal preparations. . ." Clemens, Clara, p. 35

"In June, 1835, John M. Clemens. . ." Welsh, Donald H., *Sam Clemens' Hannibal, 1836-1838 (American Studies, Vol. 3, No. 1)*, Spring 1962, p. 28-33

"The churches . . . assumed leadership. . ." Welsh, p. 28-33

"The holiday season provided a period. . ." Welsh,

p. 28-33

During the "season of fun and jollity. . ." Welsh,
    p. 28-33

"On Christmas night 150 enjoyed. . ." Welsh,
    p. 28-33

However, in Hartford, the Twain entrance hall. . .
    Floyd, "Room by Room: A Home Brought to
    Life," http://www.marktwainhouse.org/house/
    room_in_the_house.php

In the years the Clemens lived in Hartford. . . N/A,
    "Christmas with the Clemens Family," December
    23, 2009, http://marktwainhouse.blogspot.
    com/2009/12/christmas-with-clemens-family.html

The Christmas tree in the main parlor. . . N/A,
    "Christmas with the Clemens Family," December
    23, 2009, http://marktwainhouse.blogspot.
    com/2009/12/christmas-with-clemens-family.html

"Joy, and peace be with you. . ." Twain, Mark, Letter
    to Olivia Langdon Clemens, Christmas 1871

"You can't imagine how brilliant and beautiful. . ."
    Twain, Mark, Letter to William Dean Howells,
    December 1877

"The work began many weeks before the holy day. . ."

Clemens, Clara, p. 39

"Our school room provided memories. . ." Mark
Twain Library and Memorial Commission,
Mark Twain in Hartford, 1958, p. 25

"One of our cats, sarcastically called 'Apollinaris'. . ."
Clemens, Clara, p. 39

"He is very fond of animals particularly cats. . ."
Clemens, Susy, Papa, Doubleday & Co., Garden
City, NY, 1985, p. 100

"When Christmas Eve arrived at last. . ." Clemens,
Clara, p. 36

"As I often love those letters I receive. . ." Clemens,
Clara, p. 36

"We all squealed, 'Thank you. . ." Clemens, Clara,
p. 36

Palace of St. Nicholas. . . Twain, Mark, Letter to
Susy Clemens, December 25, 1875

"At this time my sisters and I. . ." Clemens, Clara, p. 36

"Ah, there they are! Rattling paper. . ." Clemens,
Clara, p. 36

"As a matter of fact, we should have been. . ."
Clemens, Clara, p. 36

"Eventually 6 A.M. came and we rang. . ." Clemens,

Clara, p. 36

"But at last each make a rush for her own table. . ."
Clemens, Clara, p. 36

"Father and Mother always rose very late. . ."
Clemens, Clara, p. 36

"When dinner parties were given. . ." Clemens,
Clara, p. 33

"I am never more tickled than when I laugh at
myself," Reid, Opie, *Mark Twain and I*, Reilly &
Lee, 1940, p. 60

"Father, however, always drew a sigh of relief. . ."
Clemens, Clara, p. 42

PART THREE: 1909—THE LAST CHRISTMAS

". . .[A]s soon as I entered this front door. . ."
Powers, p. 563

"The last thirteen days of Susy's life. . ." Clemens,
Clara, p. 50-51

"On August 15 the doctor diagnosed Susy's
illness. . ." Neider, Charles, *The Autobiography
Of Mark Twain*, Harper Perennial, New York,

1990, p. 449

"Mark Twain's eldest daughter dies. . ." Powers, p. 579

"I was standing in our dining room. . ." Powers, p. 579

"After Susy's death in 1896 it was Olivia. . ."
Floyd, "Olivia 'Livy' Langdon Clemens," http://
www.marktwainhouse.org/man/olivia_langdon_
clemens.php

"Livy died on June 5, 1904. Her death. . ." Floyd,
"Olivia 'Livy' Langdon Clemens," http://www.
marktwainhouse.org/man/olivia_langdon_
clemens.php

"She was my life, and she is gone. . ." Neider, p. 449

"We are always too busy for our children. . ." Paine,
Mark Twain: A Biography, 1835-1910, Project
Gutenberg, 2006

"He had feared for many. . ." N/A, "Miss Jean
Clemens Found Dead in Bath," *The New York
Times*, December 25, 1909

"Miss Clemens herself. . ." N/A, "Miss Jean Clemens
Found Dead in Bath," *The New York Times*,
December 25, 1909

"Never in my life before, perhaps, have I had. . ."
Shelden, Michael, *The Man in White*, Random

House, New York, NY, 2010, p. 389

"Miss Clemens went to New York. . ." N/A, "Miss Jean Clemens Found Dead in Bath," *The New York Times*, December 25, 1909

"He was not in the jovial mood so apparent. . ." Shelden, p. 388

"When I got down to Bermuda. . ." Lystra, Karen, *Dangerous Intimacy*, University of California Press, Berkley, CA, 2004, p. 245

"I am through with work for this life. . ." Lystra, p. 245

"Mark Twain today gave out the following. . ." N/A, "Twain's Merry Christmas," *The New York Times*, December 24, 1909

"My daughter was trimming. . ." N/A, "Miss Jean Clemens Found Dead in Bath," *The New York Times*, December 25, 1909

"Last night Jean, all flushed with splendid health. . ." *Paine, Mark Twain: A Biography, 1835-1910*, Project Gutenberg, 2006

"O, Clara, Clara dear, I am so glad. . ." Twain, Mark, Letter to Mrs. Clara Clemens Gabrilowitsch, December 29, 1909

Epilogue: The Gift

Today, more than 50,000 people walk through. . .
   Floyd, "Room by Room: A Home Brought to
   Life," http://www.marktwainhouse.org/house/
   room_in_the_house.php

Bibliography

BOOKS

Ayres, Alex (ed.), *The Wit and Wisdom of Mark Twain*, Harper Perennial, New York, NY, 1987

Beahrs, Andrew, *Twain's Feast*, The Penguin Press, New York, NY, 2010

Bowler, Jerry, *Santa: A Biography*, McClelland & Stewart, Toronto, Canada, 2007

Clemens, Clara, *My Father, Mark Twain*, Harper & Brothers Publishers, NY, 1931

Clemens, Susy, *Papa*, Doubleday & Co., Garden City, NY, 1985

Courtney, Steve, *The Loveliest House that Ever Was*, Dover Publications, Garden City, NY, 2011

Fisher, Henry, *Abroad with Mark Twain and Eugene Field*, West Richard, 1922

Harnsberger, Caroline Thomas, *Mark Twain at Your Finger Tips*, Dover, Mineloa, NY, 2009

Harris, Susan K., *The Courtship of Olivia Langdon and Mark Twain*, Cambridge University Press, New York, NY, 1997

Henderson, Archibald, *Mark Twain*, Echo Library, Teddington, Middlesex, UK, 2008

Hill, Hamlin, *Mark Twain: God's Fool*, Harper & Row, New York, NY, 1973

Howells, William Dean, *My Mark Twain*, Louisiana State University Press, Baton Rouge, LA, 1967

Kaplan, Fred, *The Singular Mark Twain*, Anchor Books, New York, NY, 2005

Kaplan, Justin, *Mr. Clemens and Mark Twain: A Biography*, Simon & Schuster, NY, 1966

Lystra, Karen, *Dangerous Intimacy*, University of California Press, Berkley, CA, 2004

Mark Twain Library and Memorial Commission, *Mark Twain in Hartford*, 1958

Meltzer, Milton, *Mark Twain Himself*, Wings Books, New York, NY, 1960

Neider, Charles, *The Autobiography of Mark Twain*, Harper Perennial, New York, NY, 1990

Paine, Albert Bigelow, *Mark Twain: A Biography, 1835-1910*, Project Gutenberg, 2006

Powers, Ron, *Mark Twain: A Life*, Free Press,
  New York, NY, 2005

Reid, Opie, *Mark Twain and I*, Reilly & Lee,
  1940

Shelden, Michael, *The Man in White*, Random
  House, New York, NY, 2010

Sterner, Daniel, *A Guide to Historic Hartford*,
  Connecticut, The History Press, 2012

Trombley, Laura Skandera, *Mark Twain's Other
  Woman*, Knopf, New York, NY, 2010

Twain, Mark, *Autobiography of Mark Twain, Volume
  1: The Complete and Authoritative Edition*, Edited
  by Smith, Harriet; Griffin, Benjamin; Fischer,
  Victor; Frank, Michael B.; Goetz, Sharon K.;
  Myrick, Leslie Diane, University of California,
  Berkley, CA, 2010

Twain, Mark, *The Complete Letters of Mark Twain,
  1835-1910*, Edited by Albert Bigelow Paine,
  Project Gutenberg Edition, 2006

Twain, Mark, *The Entire Project Gutenberg Works
  of Mark Twain*, Project Gutenberg, 2005

Twain, Mark, *Mark Twain's Speeches*, Create Space,
  2012

Twain, Mark, *The Wit and Wisdom of Mark Twain: A Book of Quotations* Dover, Garden City, NY, 1999

Willis, Resa, *Mark and Livy: The Love Story of Mark Twain and the Woman Who Almost Tamed Him*, Rutledge Press, New York, NY, 2003

ARTICLES

N/A, "Burglars Invade Mark Twain Villa," *The New York Times*, September 19, 1908

N/A, "Christmas with the Clemens Family," http://marktwainhouse.blogspot.com/2009/12/christmas-with-clemens-family.html

N/A, "Miss Jean Clemens Found Dead in Bath," *The New York Times*, December 25, 1909

N/A, "R.J. Collier Dies at Dinner Table," *The New York Times*, November 9, 1918

N/A, "Twain's Old Home Destroyed by Fire," *The New York Times*, July 26, 1923

Colley, Brent M., "Mark Twain's Redding, Connecticut Home: Stormfield," http://www.historyofredding.com/HRtwainstormfield.htm

Colley, Brent M., "The Story of Mark Twain's 'Christmas Elephant'," December 21, 2011, http://twainproject.blogspot.com/search?updated-min=2011-01-01T00:00:00-08:00&updated-max=2012-01-01T00:00:00-08:00&max-results=16

Dar, Bev, "Clemens' Family Christmas Described," *Courier Post* (MO), December 9, 2012

Es, Karl, "Shooting Pool with Mark Twain," *Sports Illustrated*, February 26, 1962

Floyd, Rebecca, "Olivia 'Livy' Langdon Clemens," http://www.marktwainhouse.org/man/olivia_langdon_clemens.php

Floyd, Rebecca, "Twain's Children," http://www.marktwainhouse.org/man/twains_children.php

Floyd, Rebecca, "Room by Room: A Home Brought to Life," http://www.marktwainhouse.org/house/room_in_the_house.php

Karas, Alyssa, "An Exclusive Peek of Stormfield, Twain's Last Home," November 14, 2011 http://travelingwithtwain.org/2011/11/14/redding-ct/an-exclusive-peek-of-stormfield-twains-last-home/

Mooney, Margaret; Mueller, Harold, "The History of Stormfield," http://www.marktwainlibrary.org/PDF-Files/HistoryOfStormfield.pdf

Philippon, Patti; Auerbach, Beatrice Fox, "A Home—& The Word Never Had So Much Meaning Before," http://www.marktwainhouse.org/house/history.php

Welsh, Donald H., "Sam Clemens: Hannibal 1836-1838," (American Studies, Vol. 3, No. 1), Spring 1962

Photography Credits

p. 17 Library of Congress

p. 20 Library of Congress

p. 25 Mark Twain Papers & Project at the University of California Berkeley

p. 27 Brent Colley, Mark Twain Stormfield Project

p. 34 Library of Congress

p. 36 http://commons.wikimedia.org/wiki/File:Clara_Jean_Livy_and_Susy_1880s.jpg

p. 41 Library of Congress

p. 47 http://en.wikipedia.org/wiki/File:Olivia_Langdon_Clemens,_1869.jpg

p. 52 Courtesy of the the Mark Twain Project

p. 55 Library of Congress

p. 64 Library of Congress

p. 71 Library of Congress

p. 72 Library of Congress

p. 74 Library of Congress

p. 84 Library of Congress

p. 90 Courtesy of the *Philadelphia Inquirer*, 1906

p. 91 Courtesy of *The Critic*, 1904

p. 118 Courtesy of the George Eastman House, Rochester, NY

About Cider Mill Press Book Publishers

Good ideas ripen with time. From seed to harvest, Cider Mill Press brings fine reading, information, and entertainment together between the covers of its creatively crafted books. Our Cider Mill bears fruit twice a year, publishing a new crop of titles each spring and fall.

"Where Good Books Are Ready for Press"
501 Nelson Place
Nashville, Tennessee 37214

cidermillpress.com